PERMANENTLY BARD

TONY HARRISON
PERMANENTLY BARD
Selected Poetry
EDITED BY CAROL RUTTER

BLOODAXE BOOKS

ISBN: 1 85224 262 0

First published 1995 by
Bloodaxe Books Ltd,
P.O. Box 1SN,
Newcastle upon Tyne NE99 1SN.

Bloodaxe Books Ltd acknowledges
the financial assistance of Northern Arts.

Cover printing by J. Thomson Colour Printers Ltd, Glasgow.

Printed in Great Britain by
Cromwell Press Ltd, Broughton Gifford, Melksham, Wiltshire.

To the memory of Tony's mam, Florrie Harrison,
who didn't bring up her son
'to write such mucky books'.

And to my mom, Edwardine Malley Chillington,
who brought up her daughter
to write whatever books were in her.

Acknowledgements

Most of the poetry in this book is reprinted from other publications by Tony Harrison, mainly from *Selected Poems* (Penguin Books, second edition, 1987) and *The Gaze of the Gorgon* (Bloodaxe Books, 1992). Other source texts are: *Dramatic Verse 1973-1985* (Bloodaxe Books, 1985), for *The Oresteia* and *Medea: a sex-war opera*; *V.* (Bloodaxe Books, second edition, 1989); *The Trackers of Oxyrhynchus* (Faber, 1990); *Square Rounds* and *The Common Chorus* (both Faber, 1992); and *Poetry or Bust* (Salts Estates Ltd, 1993).

For Carol Rutter's editor's acknowledgements, please see page 31.

CONTENTS

INTRODUCTION

I want to begin with four images of the poet that suggest some ways of looking at Tony Harrison. The first two are photographs in black and white. The second two aren't. They're my own memories, recorded in living colour.

The first dates from the early 1960s when Harrison was in his mid-twenties. (It appears on the cover of *The Loiners*, 1970, his first book.) It gives us the poet as Marlon Brando. Or perhaps Jimmy Porter in John Osborne's *Look Back in Anger*. (Or maybe even the 'aggro lout' Harrison will meet thirty years hence as his own alter ego in *V.*) Harrison is leaning on what ought to be a lamp-post on a street corner in Leeds, a fag dangling expertly from the hand that dangles from the arm. One leg is crossed in front of the other, casually but conspicuously bent at the knee. The denim jacket hangs open over blue jeans. It fails to conceal the chip on his shoulder that's implied in the stance. The poet is self-conscious, streetwise, brooding. He's on his own. He gazes hard at the camera, eyes narrowed – or maybe he's just squinting into the sun. It's hard to tell because the eyes are cast in shadows like the eye sockets on a Greek mask.

Still, there's something incongruously wrong with this portrait of the poet as rebel-without-a-cause. It's the hair. Brando's would have been slicked back with brilliantine. Harrison's isn't. It flops over his forehead. The flop rather spoils the effect the hard jaw-line seems to be aiming for. The flop represents a contradiction in terms, and it's suggestive. This poet is young. He's angry. And he's going to stay angry. For the next thirty years Harrison is going to write poetry that seethes with working-class aggro. It will tell the story of how, achieving one of the scholarships to Leeds Grammar School reserved in the 1940s for the plebs, he began putting 'books, books, books' between himself and his working-class parents and how, acquiring dead classical languages, he lost

> ...the tongue that once I used to know
> but can't bone up on now, and that's mi mam's.
>
> **Wordlists II**

This poet – so the photograph suggests – invites stereotypes, and he will live up to them: scholarship boy, alienated son, angry young man, self-conscious or self-mocking poet. But the flop suggests something else: that even where he invites stereotypes he's going to duck them, or throw up counter images to contest them. This will be Harrison's method: behind one image (here, the aggro pose) there will always be an incongruous counter-image (the dissident hair) that will play off the first, that will complicate it or make it a paradox. In the poetry he will achieve this superimposition by conscious design. Here, for example, is the opening of **Me Tarzan**:

> Outside the whistled gang-call, *Twelfth Street Rag*,
> then a Tarzan yodel for the kid who's bored,
> whose hand's on his liana... no, back
> to Labienus and his flaming sword.

The images that accrue over these lines superimpose Tarzan of the Apes upon Julius Caesar's general in Gaul; in one hand he seems to be clutching an epic (but exasperating: 'flaming'!) sword, in the other he's tugging at a jungle vine. But both Tarzan and Labienus turn out to be fantasies superimposed upon yet a different reality. Of a bored kid stuck in his attic garret grinding out translations of Latin prose while his mates on the street are '*off laikin''*, '*off tartin''*.

This same sort of superimposition happens in the photograph. There, it's an accident. But it's a prophetic accident. The shadow that falls behind the poet casts a monster shape on the pavement. It looks like a harpy with a fat belly and beak. What it gives us is a fantastic layering of images that make young Harrison Brando on the surface but an Aeschylean Fury just beneath. Again, this is suggestive. Harrison's poetry will habitually superimpose the modern upon the ancient, the popular upon the elite, the familiar upon the strange in layers of memory reference. And everywhere, his poetry is going to work to uncover the monsters that lurk in our lives.

In the second photograph (June 1977), the poet isn't looking at the camera. He's too busy. He's sitting on what turns out to be a rehearsal room floor: behind him a row of empty chairs sits in for an absent audience. The poet's legs are splayed out in front of him straddling a metal-studded briefcase that serves as a table, open books piled upon it three deep. Harrison's arm is raised toward his mouth. He's cupping his hand, shaping it into a megaphone. (At the same time the raised arm reveals a hole in the elbow of his jumper.) He's looking off, toward someone just out of the frame. But he's not alone in the photograph. Behind him there's an actor kneeling on a pillow in a posture that would suggest bardolatry were it not for the almost comic look of disengagement on his face. The actor isn't listening to the poet at all!

This photo locates the poet in a public space. He's stopped hanging around on street corners, marginalised. He's smack in the centre of things: the rehearsal room he's sitting in is in the National Theatre, which is itself situated at the cultural and geographic centre of the arts in Britain. This poet has found a public voice: the hand cupped into the megaphone signifies as much. It's a voice that will speak through the theatre, and over the next decade and a half, Harrison will develop into our greatest theatre poet since Shakespeare. Like Shakespeare, he will make new theatre out of re-vision: re-vision of Aeschylus' *Oresteia*, Molière's *Misanthrope*, Euripides' *Medea* and Racine's *Phèdre*. Like Shakespeare, he will construct new theatre around an ancient or legendary or historical core: **The Mysteries, The Big H, The Trackers of Oxyrhynchus, The Common Chorus, Square Rounds.**

Harrison's poetry is all, in some sense, public. It is all directed at an audience, it wants to be accessible, and even at its most inward or confessional it is dramatic and theatrical. In his sonnets, frequently two or more voices compete to be heard:

> Tugging my forelock fathoming Xenophon
> grimed Greek exams and lost me marks,
> so I whisper when the barber asks *Owt on?*
> *No, thank you!* YES! Dad's voice behind me barks.
> #### Still

In these poems soliloquy moves into dialogue and back again; a tragic (or perhaps comic or farcical) narrative develops across the sonnet sequence. The poet employs the button-holing technique of the stand-up comedian:

> No! Revolution never crossed your mind!
> #### Punchline

> Your bed's got two wrong sides. Your life's all grouse.
> #### Long Distance

> He never begged. For nowt!
> #### Turns

> My father speaking was like conjurors I'd seen...
> I'm the clown sent in to clear the ring.
> #### Fire-eater

In lines like these we hear the comedian's patter, his timing, his delivery. And his aggression. 'I went to music-hall all the time when I was a kid,' says Harrison, 'and always admired that technique of setting something up and then taking it away.' So **A Good Read** sets up Ibsen and Marx but comes down to 'You, dad'; **Still** begins with Xenophon and ends with Rudolph Valentino;

Long Distance II reacts to his dad's raw grief with a 'blight of disbelief' yet finishes with the son performing his own grief fictions. George Formby with his ukulele, 'Professor' Leon Cortez with his music-hall gags, buskers, street entertainers, and angels in white crinolines like a Gilbert and Sullivan chorus, all appear in his poetry. Secret performances become public: the mysterious plectrum the child-Harrison doesn't know the name of in **Wordlists I** but only that his father keeps it hidden in his secret condom drawer in **Punchline,** turns up, finally recognised, in *Trackers,* where Apollo uses it (unlike Tony's Dad, who never did learn) to strum the lyre.

Significantly, however, Harrison's big theatre works are not the culmination of his small-scale poetry of self and family. Quite the reverse, it was by working in the theatre, specifically on *The Oresteia,* that he found a language he could address to his parents in the sonnets. The Greeks thought of poetry as a public act which (says the Oxford Greek scholar Oswyn Murray) therefore belonged in the theatre. It was in the theatre that the 'spoken word fused with religious ritual, dance and music, to extend the boundaries of action and speech towards the unknown'. In the rhythmic pulses of verse speaking in the theatre the audience feels life upon the nerve endings: the iambic beat, says Harrison, has 'its sources in breath and blood. In the silences one should hear the heart beat.' And in the masks which Harrison and his company of actors developed to play *The Oresteia* the theatre poet discovered, paradoxically, the cover that helped uncover the private poet. He says of the Greek theatrical mask that it 'is part of the existential survival gear. It gives the bearing of survival to the actor wearing it. It represents a commitment to seeing everything through the eyes that never close. It represents a commitment to going on speaking when the always open eyes have witnessed something unspeakable. The masks must witness the unendurable. That is why they are created with their eyes open. The mouth must continue to speak in situations when the human being would be speechless or screaming and unable to articulate its agony.' After *The Oresteia,* Harrison learns to do in poetry what the masks do in theatre. The sonnets become his witness upon the unendurable, his continuous resolve to speak in situations where before he was speechless. And the learning comes too late. 'It's one of the tragic ironies of my work,' says Harrison, 'that I found a language in poetry I could address to my father and my mother only when it was too late... they're no longer around for me to address the poems to them.'

Harrison's poetry remained a closed book to his parents: 'My parents never read the poetry.' Was poetry not for the likes of them? Not up their street? Phrases like these return in the sonnets. Or was it that his mother never recovered from the shock of his first book, *The Loiners*:

> It was a library copy otherwise
> you'd've flung it in the fire in disgust.
> Even cremation can't have dried the eyes
> that wept for weeks about my 'sordid lust'.
> ...
>
> But I still see you weeping, your hurt looks:
>
> *You weren't brought up to write such mucky books!*
>
> Bringing Up

Significantly, though, 'they liked the plays'. Harrison's mother said 'maybe this is better than teaching', and she went to everything he did in the theatre. Ironic, perhaps, that the poet comes to be sitting in so exposedly public a space as a rehearsal room floor so that he can have a private conversation with his mother. Ironic, too, that the space of inclusiveness, of collaboration and team work, so ruthlessly exposes what just might wreck it: the empty seats that may not get filled, the noises off that pull focus, the spectator who should be listening but isn't, the meanness of funding for the arts that leaves holes in the poet's jumper.

The third image (December 1982) is a memory: a close-up of the poet's hands. The left hand is turned palm up, three fingers of the right hand lie across it. Below the hands, slightly out of focus in my memory-image, is a bulging album-sized book, opened at random. It is the poet's workbook, a literary version of a Renaissance collectanea or cabinet of curiosities. Or maybe it's a material re-collection of his own childhood. 'In our street,' says Harrison, 'every kind of cultural throwaway from spring-cleaned attics and the cellars of the deceased found its way to me': 'piles of old 78s, George Formby, the Savoy Orpheans, Sophie Tucker... and sometimes the odd book, an old guide to Matlock...a Livingstone's *Travels* so massive I could barely manhandle it.'

The workbook is a mind file. Stuck to its pages are postcards, news clippings, photographs, quotations: Lyndon Johnson, Margaret Thatcher, Arthur Scargill, the Pope, Kate Millett; extracts from a treatise on Aristophanic comedy, another on sixteenth-century English rhetoric. There are aeroplane tickets to destinations in Livingstone's book, cartoons, maps, snatches of poetry retrieved from 520 BC or 1520 AD. There are drafts of new poetry. And pictures, pictures, pictures. An aerial shot of the theatre at Epidaurus faces a photo of women shaking the perimeter fences at Greenham Common. A Frenchman in black dressed up as a skeleton faces a row of black tribal faces, ritually painted in intricate designs like bones. The workbook – he compiles a series of them for every project – is the book that Harrison puts together as he's putting together the images that will make the poetry. Everywhere the book bears the marginal notation of the poet, his captions or comments in that unmistakable handwriting that looks like chicken feet in English but in Greek has the shapeliness of patterns decorating a wine jar. Everything interests this poet, particularly the quirky puns or rhymes he keeps observing in culture-at-large, the way, for instance, a 'V' for 'versus' aerosoled onto a gravestone might be made into 'verses' or the graffiti 'United' read both as the football team and post-mortem reunion.

In the image I am focusing on, however, the workbook is in the background. My close-up is on the hands. This poet, my image wants to say, is a manual labourer. He is a word-wright. He is of the working class. The material he works in is words. His workbooks, the works *literally* of his hands, are to this poet what his baker-father's loaves were.

As the poet talks, his hands work. The fingers of the right hand move round and round in circles on the palm of the left. These working hands may be a paradox, for poetry is 'sedentary toil' says Yeats: 'difficulty is our plough'. Typically, though, Harrison thinks not of the plough but of the *mill* when he finds a metaphor for his own tenacious word-work: 'monstrous North of England millstone grit'. Some of his sonnets have been through fifty revisions. So the poet's hands go on rubbing, rubbing, rubbing. He might be rubbing the millstones. Or rubbing butter into flour. Or poetry into shape.

In my final image, another memory (September 1993), the poet is standing on a red carpet. He's been there before. He's had premières in New York and London. Bizarrely, though, here in Bradford he's standing on the red carpet *pushing a hoover*. Behind him, shrouded in drapes that make them ghosts, are the busts of England's greatest poets. Milton. Keats. Shakespeare. Harrison is not out of place. For a time he works among them, keeping his head down. He's intent upon removing all the footprints the actors – who've gone off for a cup of tea before premièring this latest Harrison, *Poetry or Bust* – have tracked onto the carpet.

It's hard to imagine Milton doing the hoovering. Or even Shakespeare, though like Harrison he was a working-class grammar-school lad, a word-wright.

Occupied with his task in the (almost) deserted playing space, the poet is oblivious of the incongruous spectacle he presents, the living bard backed by the dead, every one of them a conversationalist in the running dialogue Harrison keeps up with them about the making of poetry, the uses of poetry, the ends (or end) of poetry. The man behind the hoover gives us the poet as domestic, doing "woman's work", attending to the humble. The gender confusion of the moment is suggestive. Harrison makes no grand claims for poetry. He grew up in an environment where poetry was only for the 'lassy lad', where *Miles* (the soldier) and *Mercator* (the merchant) were elevated into icons of approved masculine aspiration in the chapel windows of his grammar school but *Poeta* (the Latin even *sounds* cissy!) didn't get a look-in. Part of Harrison scorns Shelley's idealisation of the poet as the 'unacknowledged legislator of the world' and replies, with Auden, that 'poetry makes nothing happen'. But another part of him makes the journey with Dionysus in Aristophanes' *Frogs* to the underworld to bring a poet back to life. Why? 'To save the city of course.' And just as Harrison feels self-division – 'my head faces human history and has a very bleak and pessimistic view of the possibilities for mankind' while his heart's an optimist, entertaining a 'celebratory nature' – so he feels artistic division. What can the poet do to repair the horrors of the late twentieth century – Auschwitz, Hiroshima, reigns of terror and acid rain – when 'This pen's all I have of magic wand'?

Yet this poet *does* make reparation. Observing in history a continuous programme of genocide effected by the silencing of individuals and classes oppressed into inarticulacy by ignorance, or patriarchy, or the drudgery of over-work, Harrison, the poet, speaks for the speechless. 'The dumb go down in history and disappear', but the poet gives them a voice.

He puts the inarticulate on record: his Uncle Harry, a deaf-mute; the stammerer, Uncle Joe; his father, who was 'kept...down' by a 'tongue that weighed like lead'; a nameless convict who, to settle the toffs' wager, was winched into a bottomless pit and brought back 'flayed, grey, mad, dumb'; the skinhead dole-wallah who defaces tombstones with 'V' and himself with tattoos; the Iraqi soldier immolated in his tank, his charred lips half-open; Iphigeneia, Agamemnon's daughter, 'hoisted like a goat to the godstone, a gag in her mouth' so she cannot curse as her throat is cut and the sacrifice made so the Greek ships can sail for Troy.

Speaking for the speechless, it turns out that Harrison is speaking for himself. He is a ventriloquist who puts words into his *own* mouth. For he was the schoolboy made to 'shut my trap' by the sarcasm of the English teacher who, when he recited Keats, mocked his accent and called him 'barbarian':

> 4 words only of *mi 'art aches* and ... 'Mine's broken,
> you barbarian, T.W.!' *He* was nicely spoken.
> 'Can't have our glorious heritage done to death!'

> I played the Drunken Porter in *Macbeth*.

> 'Poetry's the speech of kings. You're one of those
> Shakespeare gives the comic bits to: prose!'
> **Them & [uz]**

And he was the son who sat silent in those silent family teas where the only sound was

> ...father's celery, the clock's loud tick,
> the mine subsidence from deep underground,
> mi mam's loose bottom teeth's relentless click.
> **Illuminations IV**

And he was the 'scholar' who'd acquired five languages but couldn't put anything into words at his mother's funeral or find words down the telephone until his father was dead and the phone disconnected. 'I've got to find the right words on my own,' he silently answers his father's chivvying in **Book Ends II**, and his poetry documents that search. The poet in these poems is tongue-tied; he stammers, he chews, he hawks up 'great lumps' of 'glottals' to 'spit out'; his poetry glugs 'like poured pop'; it 'thickens to a lumpen mass'. A fellow poet, Blake Morrison, observes Harrison's 'clumping rhymes, the all-too-iambic pentameters, the sheer confusion of layout and typography, as capitals, italics, Latin and Greek tags, brand-names, songs, advertising jingles, dictionary symbols and dialect rub shoulders on pages that have no pagination'. We observe most of this in **Them & [uz]**, which begins in Greek and ends:

> All poetry (even Cockney Keats?) you see
> 's been dubbed by [ʌs] into RP,
> Received Pronunciation, please believe [ʌs]
> your speech is in the hands of the Receivers.'

> 'We say [ʌs] not [uz], T.W.!' That shut my trap.
> I doffed my flat a's (as in 'flat cap')
> my mouth all stuffed with glottals, great
> lumps to hawk up and spit out... *E-nun-ci-ate!*

Blake Morrison comments: 'these must be some of the least fluent poems in the language'. And this is the point. 'They mean to be.' Because they are trying to 'find the right words on my own'. It's a tongue-tied, stuttering business.

If it is true, as he has been known to claim, that all Harrison's poetry is an act of slow revenge upon that original English teacher, it is also true that the poet who's spoiling for a fight, the Brando lookalike, is the same poet who's pushing the hoover and who finds his punch in his punch line. Observe: for this poet who does his work with words, the knuckleduster that his grandfather carried everywhere 'just in case', that 'knuckleduster's now [his] paperweight!'

* * *

The poetry selected in *Permanently Bard* is arranged in five sections. Section One serves as an introduction. It begins with the four-line poem **Heredity** which answers those who ask the poet who his "influences" were and want him to answer 'Yeats' or 'Pound': someone "highbrow". This deceptively mild little statement manages to radiate social rage even as it contains it. It lays out Harrison's recurrent theme, the repression of working-class speech. It suggests a (valid) connection between articulation and power on the one hand and a (spurious) connection between poetry – as elitist cultural property – and class on the other.

Thomas Campey and the Copernican System picks up on these ideas. It introduces the bibliophile rag-and-bone man who, dragging a hand-cart through Leeds collecting the debris of house clearances and spring cleanings, dragged to market books that equipped the young Harrison with his first ' "gentleman's" library'. The point the poem makes is political – and tells against the poet. Thomas Campey does not read the books whose weight on his cart bends his spine into a twisted question mark. He's one of those 'clowns' – like the satyrs who hold up the stage at the theatre of Dionysus – whose backs are broken under a culture they never get to share. Yet the question Campey's crippled body asks follows the poet everywhere: a line drawing of Campey figures as the motif on the poet's own bookplate (reproduced on page 32). Every time Harrison opens a book, he meets Campey.

The final poem in this section – really a pair of sonnets – is what I think of as Harrison's "manifesto". Its title – **Them & [uz]** – is class-conscious and polemical (he uses the phonetic alphabet here to represent his Yorkshire [uz]). The poem's divisions polarise around

17

those plural pronouns of inclusion and exclusion, but the [uz] is branded with a class accent that limits its inclusiveness, and the excluded 'Them' is yet connected to [uz] with the ampersand (&). The poem proceeds by a series of paradoxical and revealing juxtapositions. In the opening line, the 'αἰαῖ' in Greek is the plangent lament of the tragic chorus, but it is shoved up against the chirpy 'ay ay!' which sounds just like it but happens to be the signature phrase of the stand-up comic 'Professor' Leon Cortez. "Elitist" and "popular" culture stand cheek by jowl in this poem which works utterly to erase such divisions between "high" and "low" art as are being artificially set up by the mindlessness of English teachers – guardians of "literature" – like the one portrayed here. So the scholarship boy with the Leeds accent who will go on to translate Aeschylus is stopped by the teacher from reading Keats because we 'Can't have our glorious heritage done to death': all poetry, says the teacher, has been 'dubbed by [ʌs] into RP,/ Received Pronunciation'. What the scholarship boy discovers, though, is that John Keats had a Cockney accent, and Wordsworth made straight rhymes of 'matter' and 'water'. Poetry it seems has been 'dubbed' in more than one sense! But no longer. In the second sonnet, the voice that was relegated to 'the comic bits... prose' claims poetry; he claims a seat in the School of Eloquence. [uz] is here to stay in poetry that uses 'my name and own voice'; 'the language that I spoke at home'. However, like those music-hall comics whose technique Harrison so admires, this second sonnet sets up one thing only to take it away: the working-class poet claims his voice and name. He declares his rights. He announces his manifesto. Yet somehow cultural elitism manages to recapture him. His first notice in the "high art" *Times* assumes his 'Tony' must be 'Anthony' and so corrects the name his mother gave him.

The poems in Section Two are arranged chronologically. This is tricky, though, for just as Harrison frequently puts two or three voices in a poem, so he puts two or three times in a poem, or a sequence of times that slide across each other anachronistically. In **Isolation** for example, his father's bleating grief (in the present?) is set against his mother's funeral (that morning?) and the train journey he took (yesterday?) to get there for it, which triggers the memory – and this is where the poem *starts* – of another isolation when, aged seven, he was taken from his mother to be quarantined in the scarlet fever hospital:

> I cried once as a boy when I'd to leave her
> at Christmas in the fourth year of the War,

taken to Killingbeck with scarlet fever,
but don't cry now, although I see once more
from the window of the York-Leeds diesel back
for her funeral, my place of quarantine,

...

and don't, though the fresh grave's flecked with sleet,
and dad, with every fire back home switched on, 's
frozen,
    and don't,
        until I hear him bleat
round the ransacked house for his long johns.

The poems of Section Two are biographical but also elegiac: they
mourn the silences never filled, the connections never made. The
elegy in Harrison's hands has a hard political edge to it, for silence
is class oppression and the process of language acquisition is a
process of division. These poems are about separation from family,
from friends, from class. So the kid who'd really like to be Tarzan
swinging from the trees instead sweats in his attic translating
Caesar's *Wars in Gaul* while his mates on the street are *'off laikin'*
... off tartin', off to t'flicks'. And the wet-behind-the-ears-and-oh-
so-pretentious scholarship boy who stands on the pier at Blackpool
gripping hands with his parents still manages to demonstrate how
much distance there is between them:

...some days ended up all holding hands
gripping the pier machine that gave you shocks.
The current would connect. We'd feel the buzz
ravel our loosening ties to one tense grip,
the family circle, one continuous US!

But 'that was the first year on my scholarship', so the show-off
'scholar' had to lecture

them on neutrons and Ohm's law
and other half-baked Physics I'd been taught.

It was he with his education who would interrupt the 'one contin-
uous US!':

I'd be the one who'd make that circuit short.

Illuminations II

These poems are like high-definition snapshots in a family album.
There's Uncle Joe, who compensated for his stammer by hand-
setting printer's type faster than he could talk. There's mute Uncle
Harry, stabbing the dictionary for words. Grandpa Horner, who
pulped a sewer rat with his boot. Grandpa Harrison, the publican,
who paid for his beer in guineas. Dad, the baker, icing sand-castles

on Blackpool beach like cakes for the tide to eat; poring over his Leeds United programme while his son read Kafka; mocking the boy as 'Paganinny' when his art-aspiring hair fell over his collar; warming his wife's slippers by the fire though she'd been two years dead; grousing about the food, the diabetes, the neighbourhood 'gone Pakki'; dropping dead beside the post-box, his flat cap inside up beside him as though he were busking. And Mam. Who started the poetry: 'simple rhymes...at her knee...that began when her lap was warm, with ABC'. But this Mam would have thrown her son's first book – *The Loiners* – into the fire if it hadn't been a library copy brought round by a neighbour. And so, instead, she wept her disgust:

> *You weren't brought up to write such mucky books!*
> Bringing Up

There is love in these sonnets. The choc-ice his father slips into his hand as the Cagney film starts is a love token. So is the apple pie baked on the day his mother dropped dead. There is a great deal of humour in these sonnets. Harrison's wit is mordant and he sometimes makes you laugh out loud. But more often there is derision and incomprehension in the poems: *'Wi' 'air like that you ought to wear a skirt!'* jeers his dad. And the boy jeers back: 'Good read! I bet!...The labels on your whisky or your beer.' Only belatedly does understanding come: the son finally comprehends the mystery of his father's obsession with brilliantine when he sees a photograph of Rudolph Valentino and discovers who his father was trying to be.

In all of these sonnets-as-family-snapshots, the son is present. Sullen, grudging, reticent, he's somewhere in the corner. His growth into poetry, into articulacy, is what finally conquers the son's reticence. He who muttered to himself or through clenched teeth in the poems of Section Two gains a wider audience in Section Three where **Classics Society**, **National Trust** and **Rhubarbarians** show him exploring the politics of speech in a social context. The divisions he's thinking of in these poems are historic, economic, social: 'our leaders', the 'stout upholders of our law and order', 'the gaffers' – possessers of the right to speech – are set against the dispossessed: the 'delinquent', the 'convict', 'the mob', who, dumb, 'go down in history and disappear'. **Divisions** sees how contemporary society is reproducing the same old disenfranchisements in the same old ways: the tattooed skinheads the poet meets in the baths have no voice in town hall or Whitehall; they make their subversive mark on the surfaces they have to hand, graffitiing subway walls and their own skins.

20

In the three **Art & Extinction** sonnets, the poet considers whether *the poet* will follow the others down the hole of history. Standing in front of a glass case displaying 'The Earth's Endangered Species' in an international airport heaving with humanity (some of it intent on making its lesser species extinct by killing their language), the poet sees himself reflected in the glass and so reflects upon *his* chances of survival. Will the poet, like the long-haired mammoth, be lost, only 'preserved beneath deep permaverse'? And if the species is doomed to extinction, what about language? Is the poet a cannibal of language or a conservationist? 'By using them do we save words or not?' Two poems in this section look at these dark issues from a comic perspective. **Summoned by Bells** reflects wryly upon a society driving itself mad with the alarm bells it installs to make secure the material stuff it doesn't need. And **Y** (we hear the title as 'Why?') observes that even on aeroplanes the British mark their class divisions.

The poems of these first three sections go round and round the same topics. (I think of the millstone grinding, the poet's hands rubbing.) They are intensely emotional, but almost never sentimental. An austere aesthetic informs and restrains them. Harrison was, after all, trained up on the disciplines of the classics. Virgil, Horace, Ovid, Martial, Aeschylus, Euripides, Sophocles, Sappho were his tutors, and they taught him to confine wild emotion in forms that make its expression communicable.

The technical virtuosity he learned from such tutors is striking. Harrison writes formally, metrically, and in rhyme. His typical line moves like a pugilist: muscular, vigorous, punchy. It plays the feint. It's quick on its feet. Harrison calls metre in poetry 'a life support system. A strong rhythm is necessary for me because those strong rhythms mean the appetite for life.' The metre allows the poet to explore danger, to 'go closer to the fire, deeper into the darkness' because it carries him through it: 'I don't have the heart to confront some experience unless I know I have this rhythm to carry me to the other side.' The iambic pulse (de *dum* de *dum*) is the human pulse – and the human impulse – of the heart that keeps on beating.

One poetic form that Harrison keeps returning to regularly is the sonnet: 'I write sonnets fairly continuously – like someone tapping a barometer.' Again, the form holds the emotion together, makes it transmissible: 'It's like giving blood. If you're dying I can't give you blood by slashing my wrists; it has to go through a sterile jar.' Poetic form is that sterile jar. He uses a sixteen-line sonnet form (the one George Meredith used in his sonnet-novel, *Modern Love*) not Shakespeare's fourteen-line form. He favours it for its malleability: 'you can make it do what the traditional octet-sestet fourteener can do', presenting one idea or situation in the first, longer part of the poem then contradicting it or reversing it in the second, or suddenly turning the whole poem in the couplet. But 'you can also use it as two octets so that the dialectic is stronger, and it has strong narrative possibilities when you use it as four quatrains'. Harrison frequently breaks the sonnet apart into contrapuntal voices (where the italic type face designates other voices than the poet's – a teacher, George Formby, a Lakeland paperhanger, his dad). Or he hives off single lines, his punch lines.

Poetic form, however, is not, for Harrison, something to be imposed. It is something to be discovered. 'It's not a question of taking something and putting it into some container; it's a question of finding out what that something is. Which comes out through finding the form.' Harrison says of rhyme: 'It's not a restrictive thing, it's actually an instrument of discovery. Because the associations' – that happen through rhyme – 'are sometimes irrational, it keeps the subject in focus in a molten state. It doesn't set too soon.'

But what is wonderful about Harrison's poetic formalism is the way it is used to carry the language of everyday speech: the form is learned, but the speech itself is colloquial. The critic Damian Grant hits on this when he speaks of Harrison's 'confident switches of linguistic register', 'the classical and the colloquial assorting together', and of 'his skilful rhyming (like a shotgun marriage) of the elevated word with the demotic, "RP" [Received Pronunciation] with dialect, English with other languages.'

Most skilfully of all – and most dangerously, for the shotgun gives way to precision sniper fire – this poet is a punster. Puns are acts of linguistic subversion. They bring together ideas normally kept apart and, making identical twins of them to the ear, let them clown around, but always with the threat of releasing havoc. Like guerrilla gorillas on the loose, where the monkeys might at any time start lobbing grenades. Puns are more than intellectual teases. In Harrison's repertoire, they make political connections. The schoolboy who reads Cicero when he could be '*off tartin*' ' is a 'Cissy-ro'; the long hair the young poet affects makes him a 'Paganinny'. A 'gob' is a mouth but also a worked-out seam of coal. The dumb go 'down' in history. 'Aspiration' – ambition – manifests itself in 'aspiration' – pronouncing your h's. You drop a class if you drop an h. You 'rifle' a dictionary because it's a 'bible paper bomb'. You prove you're a man when you drink yourself 'legless'. '*Tabes dorsalis*' is wastage of the spine. It's the disease that afflicts Thomas Campey, the man who spends his life collecting waste paper and books he'll never read. His life is a waste. And wasted. 'D' in **Marked with D.** belongs to the pat-a-cake rhyme, the 'baker's man' rhyme. It stands for 'Dad'. But also for 'Death' and 'Dunce'. The fire the bakerman stokes is his bread oven. But it's also the fire that burned Troy, the ovens of Auschwitz, and the crematorium that reduces him, finally, to ash. 'Illuminations' are the lights of Blackpool's pleasure beach. And they're sudden recognitions. And, on a medieval manuscript, they're the miniature paintings that decorate the initial letter of a text. 'Dividers' are a draughtsman's instruments and class divisions, divisions that get reproduced in football divisions.

Harrison's puns are only one manifestation of what he calls his 'obsession with language'. Coming from a background where there were no books, and living among people who felt themselves to be inarticulate, Harrison was 'voraciously obsessive about acquiring language and power over language, both other languages and the language of poetry, which is still to me language at its most powerful, expressive and ceremonious'. He quotes Arthur Scargill at the beginning of *V.*, his meditation upon the vandalised cemetery where his parents' tombstone has been aerosoled with four-letter words by graffiti "artists" who seem to have no other access to language than the spray can: 'My father still reads the dictionary every day,' says Scargill. 'He says your life depends on your power to master words.' Harrison's mute Uncle Harry would have agreed. His *Funk & Wagnalls* dictionary was his bible and his bomb. He

> jabbed at its lexis till it leaped to life
> when there were Tory errors to confute.
>
> **Wordlists II**

Harrison treats words like objects. They have weight and shape and density. They savour to the palate. They are delicate. They delight. He turns them over in his hands. He tastes them in his mouth. He takes them apart: why is history not her/story? That's a question he pursues in *The Oresteia* where it's Helen of Troy and her/story that get taken apart:

> HELEN wrecker HELEN Hell...
> HEL- spear-bride gore-bride war whore -EN
>
> **from *The Oresteia***

He puts new words together: 'Littererchewer'. He renovates clichés: 'wish you were here'; 'chilled to the bone'; 'the penny dropped'. He combines old words into new compounds to make new, multi-referential meanings. 'Cissy-bleeding-ro' in **Me Tarzan** is one example. 'Rhubarbarians' in the poem so titled is another.

Harrison is a poet who makes us interested in words. He sends us to dictionaries to look words up: 'glossolalia', 'duciloquy'. He uses strange words: 'Ormus', 'Ind'. He makes us take another look at words we thought we knew: 'name', 'art', 'black'. He moves fluently between registers of language. He puts a local Leeds word next to a Latinate word Milton would have used. Words we trot out only for special occasions – galas, funerals, rituals of life and death – Harrison harnesses to language that kicks around in the gutter. His poems move fluently between languages. They speak Greek, Latin, French, Czech, Spanish, Swahili.

The point is not to mystify or to exclude. Harrison never claims an "elevated" or "restricted" or "appropriate" language for poetry. Quite the reverse. He claims *all* language for poetry. When he writes 'αἰαῖ, ay, ay!' at the beginning of **Them & [uz]** he's demonstrating that the Greek tragic theatre and the English music hall use the *same*, not different, categories of language. The Latin Caesar spoke was demotic (= 'of the people'); the Greek Aeschylus wrote was colloquial (= 'belonging to the common speech'). All language is right for [uz], and all language is right for poetry. So these poems require us to wrap our tongues round Greek and Cornish and Elizabethan English. As we do so, they empower us. Through them we claim the power over and with language that matters so much to Harrison.

Likewise, though, these poems require us to speak 'rhubarb'. That is, they make us speak like Loiners, in dialect:

> *Ah bloody can't ah've gorra Latin prose.*
> **Me Tarzan**

> *Wi' 'air like that you ought to wear a skirt!*
> **An Old Score**

> *Ah've allus liked things sweet! But now ah push
> food down mi throat! Ah'd sooner do wi'out.*
> **Long Distance I**

The poems make us rhyme 'us' with 'buzz'. They make us use the tongue – 'mi mam's' – that Harrison says he 'can't bone up on now' and yet constantly reverts to. This language, too, is power.

The public voice the poet finds in the poems in Section Three of this book is explored and amplified in Section Four, in poems that stretch back to Harrison's earliest memories then circle round to his most recent concerns. Extracts from the theatre poetry figure here, but the section is introduced with the **Sonnets for August 1945** and the Gulf War poem **Initial Illumination**. The recurrent image of the circle – which began in the family sonnets with rings that survived the fire (like his mother's 'eternity' ring, his father's family ring) – connects all this poetry.

The circle appears first as a circle of fire, then as a circle of scorched cobblestones, then of packed earth. It is the fireball over Hiroshima. It is the shape left in tar after a celebration bonfire. It is the dancing floor of the Greek theatre. It is the 'O' a snake curls into swallowing its tail, or a satyr's lips make, forming around Athene's flute, or an arms manufacturer specifies, designing artillery rounds.

The circle takes Harrison back to first memories. 'When I search my memory for something to explain what drove me into poetry, my images are all to do with the War... bombs falling, the windows shaking, myself and my mother crouching in the cellar listening.' Those memories trigger the next: of 'a street party with bonfires and such joy, celebration and general fraternity as I have never seen since, with normally taciturn people laughing, singing and dancing at the end of a terrible war. Furniture was brought out of the houses to keep the blaze going. The fire became so high the telephone wires were burned down. The paint on our back gate blistered and peeled off. It went on all night and in the morning I helped to douse the fire and shovel the ashes into tea chests to be taken away. When the space was cleared the celebratory bonfire had left a black circle of scorched cobbles with thick scars of tar.'

Only later did he connect this celebration with the suffering that lay behind it, the atom bomb dropped on Hiroshima. The fire of celebration, the terrible fire of annihilation, and the circle: 'one space for the celebrant and the sufferer'. And only later still did the poet learn to give another name to that circle, to call it 'orchestra' – the Greek word meaning 'circular dancing place' – and to people that place with celebrants and sufferers who were as dazed and dumbfounded by the circle, the cycle, of human violence in Athens in 500 BC as the child Harrison had been in Leeds in 1945.

All of the poetry in this section is war poetry. The Chorus of Old Men from *Agamemnon* (the first play in the *Oresteia Trilogy*) tells the story of the war in Troy, the war for 'one woman, the whore war'. It is a war that requires the killing of one woman – Iphigeneia – so that another – Helen – can be saved. Or is it male ego that must be saved? This irony is lost on those 'Argos geezers' who tell the story. And yet, in **The Ballad of the Geldshark**, the Old Men ventriloquise women's voices and are able to count the appalling cost of war to the survivors. 'Where's my father   husband boy?' they ask. And they answer:

> give to WAR your men's fleshgold
> and what are your returns?
> kilos of cold clinker packed
> in army-issue urns.

When the Herald enters, his crowing speech begins with a glorification of male adventurism: 'I doubt raper Paris thought it was worth it'. But then, getting on to the suffering, the death, the speech turns bleak. War is waste:

> the best lads in their tonloads tangled and landed
> and gashed by the flesh-hook, the fish-gaff of Ares.

The part Clytemnestra – wife of Agamemnon, mother of Iphigeneia – plays in all this is (subversively, fatally) to interrogate male practice. What's the difference between slaughter – war that valorises men as heroes – and slaughter – murder that pollutes and maddens them? There is no difference, says the mother, so she carries the grudge of the child-killing under her heart until her husband returns triumphant from Troy. Then she hacks him down in his bath.

Lysistrata asks similar questions about masculine investment in war in *The Common Chorus*, Harrison's re-vision of Aristophanes' comedy which has the women of Athens going on a sex strike as the only way of bringing men to their senses to stop the war that is killing them all. Harrison's play is set at Greenham Common where the god Poseidon of Aristophanes returns as the Poseidon nuclear missile. 'Mrs Strata' tries to beat into the Inspector's head the evident truth that war is a game boys can no longer afford to play or that women can afford to let them play. In the extract from *Square Rounds*, Clara Haber, the chemist, has the same argument with her husband Fritz, the brilliant Jewish scientist who invents chemical warfare for the German Kaiser in World War I to counter an earlier generation's ultimate weapon of death, the Puckle gun. The gun, a brilliant piece of war technology, is a product of European civilisation that preserves the white man's cultural superiority even in killing. It shoots "humane" round rounds at Germans, but mutilating 'square rounds' at "savages". Haber defends the superior technology of *his* new ultimate weapon – killer gas – because it leaves corpses intact. Mothers will have bodies to bury instead of mangled meat. Clara predicts a future in which the Kaiser's gas invented by the Jew will be used against the Jew. Then she stops talking. She blows her head off.

The *Medea* Chorus tells us to keep on talking. The war these women are concerned with is the sex war, what Friedrich Engels called 'the historical defeat of the female sex'. 'Keep women down' was allegedly the third inscription on Apollo's temple at Delphi, along with 'Know thyself' and 'Nothing too much'. To 'keep women down' men have supplanted the ancient matriarchal earth-gods with a new race of patriarchal sky-gods, born of intellect, not blood: so much tidier! And they have hi-jacked myth to rewrite it to validate his/tory. But the *Medea* Chorus tells the unreconstructed truth. Medea didn't kill her children, as the male myth would have it. It was men who did the killing. The men of Corinth stoned the children.

The connection between art and violence – the art of the soldier, the art of the chemist, the art of the poet turning war into art – is explored most feelingly by Silenus in the extract from *The Trackers of Oxyrhynchus*, the play Harrison wrote around the only surviving Sophoclean fragment of a Greek satyr play. We know that Greek tragedy always took the form of a trilogy performed on a single day, *followed* by a fourth play, a satyr play, written, says Harrison, 'by the same author, with a Chorus of what we can see as men in their animal condition, represented as half or three quarters men with horse or goat attributes and an erect phallus'. The satyr play is bawdy, gross, raucous, insubordinate. And it co-exists with the tragedy. It releases the audience into celebration undefeated by the tragic. But as early as the third century BC these satyr plays were being destroyed – perhaps systematically, perhaps by neglect – by the compilers of the great library in Alexandria, whose refinement felt that the gross cavortings of stiff-penised "low art" satyrs were ill-sorted to the "high art" emotions of tragedy. Silenus in *Trackers* narrates this history. He tells what satyrs are, what they do. And what they don't do. For one thing, they hold up the stage of Dionysus, but they never step on it. Their role is to 'wonder' but never to perform. Telling the appalling story of Marsyas, Silenus tells how art has been divided into 'high' and 'low' and the high ground appropriated by totalitarian Apollo and his priests.

The final extract in this section, from *Poetry or Bust*, shifts the debate about art, poetry, culture and death back into the domestic setting. John Nicholson, the self-acclaimed Airedale poet, goes to London to have himself immortalised in marble. But the bust he can afford is only plaster. And while he goes on a bender, drinking his little fame, his baby dies of starvation. What can he make of her now, demands his wife. 'A poem by John Nicholson?' That's meant to be a blow. But Nicholson takes it like an artist. His dead child is indeed transformed into a poem. (Nicholson is the 'permanently barred' bard who contributes the title of this book.)

In Harrison's work it is in the theatre poetry that the woman's voice speaks most clamorously. His family poems may reek of testosterone and privilege the male voice, but the theatre poetry claims space for the female. It shows that mankind is doomed if it will not listen to the voice of the woman. For men, 'coming to terms with one's female qualities seems to be a very necessary struggle,' Harrison says. 'You learn to do that by loving.' The theatre poetry is all about *wrecked* love. But it is yet part of our struggle – *agon* is the Greek word – to learn.

The final group of poems in *Permanently Bard* returns the poet to his meditations upon poetry through a number of ghostly conversations he has with other poets. **A Kumquat for John Keats** finds in that fruit whose inside is bitter, its outside sweet – or is it the other way around? – a perfect metaphor for joy in a world of pain, the Melancholy, Keats said, that dwells inside Delight. **Remains** puns on what survives and what, as 'last remains' won't, to look behind the shutter in Wordsworth's Grasmere cottage and to discover a secret line of poetry. **The Call of Nature** sees versions of those rubber-necks who 'traipse round Wordsworth's lakeland shrine' descend by the busload upon D.H. Lawrence's New Mexico where the native Pueblo Indians who live there play themselves in films that travesty them, where kitsch defaces the landscape, and where tourists only seek out Lawrence because they've heard of his reputation as the high priest of serious sex – while their own sex is travestied, cutely kitschified on toilet doors.

On Not Being Milton, the last poem in this collection, summarises, recaps and takes us back to the book's beginning. It is Harrison's *'Cahier d'un retour au pays natal'* – his notes on his return to his native land. It can be read as a gloss on all the poetry. Indeed, it might stand, as it does in *Continuous* – Harrison's collected sonnets – as the first poem in this book. In **Milton**, Harrison takes up the cause of inarticulacy: 'Three cheers for mute ingloriousness.' He wants language to be, in his hands, like the Enoch hammer the Luddites used to smash the frames of machinery that threatened to dispossess them of labour as they'd already been dispossessed of language by 'the frames of Art'. Paradoxically, this championing of the inarticulate ('Articulation is the tongue-tied's fighting') is itself 'framed' in so consciously literate a form that it threatens to exclude the very people whose interests it offers to serve. All of that, though, is undone in the final line of the poem, which is also the final line of this book. '*Sir, I Ham a very Bad Hand at Righting*' – quoting the Cato Street conspirator, Tidd – is yet a final instance of the poet ventriloquising 'mute ingloriousness'. Insofar as the line completes the idea introduced in the poem's title, **On Not Being Milton**, it ironises it by reversing it. Clearly, Tony Harrison is a *dab* 'Hand at Righting'.

* * *

Permanently Bard is a selection of Harrison's work. There is much *more* Harrison, his work for television, for example, which depends so much on the close reading of visual against verbal image that it has not been possible to represent it here: **Black Daisies for the Bride, The Gaze of the Gorgon, The Blasphemer's Banquet.** There are some obvious omissions that serious students of Harrison will want to pursue: longer poems such as **A Cold Coming** and *V.*

Wherever you find Harrison, though, he will be 'permanently bard', always the poet, for 'poetry is all I write'. Whether for television, for theatre, for film, for the opera house, for daily newspapers, for collected or selected works, Harrison writes only poetry. It is a poetry some audiences find so controversial that for them Harrison the 'bard' is 'permanently *barred*': when *V.* was televised by Channel 4 the censorious wanted it banned. Poetry hit the front page of the newspapers. Poetry even had questions asked about it in Parliament. Not bad for a bard!

Reading this selection it is perhaps useful to keep in mind the image Harrison invents in **Wordlists I** of a gauge, one end marked 'words', the other 'wordlessness' with an arm swinging between them going 'almost ga-ga'. Harrison's poetry isn't made up of contradictions. It is made up of points upon a gauge. It has a huge range and tolerance. Sometimes the swings go 'almost ga-ga'. Harrison himself calls poetry 'the heartless art': as John Nicholson in *Poetry or Bust* so heartlessly shows, poetry uses life as its 'material'. Yet Harrison's poetry is full of heart: it is striking, indeed, how often Harrison puns 'art' and 'heart', which are of course both ''art' in Leeds dialect. Again, Harrison's poetry is committed to speech. It gives 'mute ingloriousness' a voice. Yet Harrison cites the poet Hieronymus Frascatorious, who was 'born, as perhaps befits a true poet, without a mouth' and died 'after an apoplexy, speechless.' This *speechless* Frascatorious, says Harrison, is 'almost the sort of poet I think I am'!

So what can I say about the 'very Bad Hand at Righting'? There's no debate about that one at all. Or about the wrighting. Or writing.

CAROL RUTTER

EDITOR'S ACKNOWLEDGEMENTS

Teachers get a bad press in Tony Harrison's poetry, but it is merely the truth to say that *Permanently Bard* could not have been written without the collaboration of several remarkable English teachers. Dave Cath, Jonathan Ward, and Adrian Beard – all passionate about Harrison's poetry – shared their expertise with me unstintingly. They advised me on the selection of the poetry, made suggestions about presentation and format, supplied additional material, read drafts and redrafts and commented on those drafts at length and with huge enthusiasm. In a real sense, they have been my tutors, and in the time-honoured tradition of tutorials, I have cribbed their best ideas. Another teacher, Erika Denham, who 'discovered' Harrison the morning his Gulf War poem *A Cold Coming* appeared in *The Guardian*, shared with me an article she had written for sixth form teachers wanting to introduce Harrison's poetry. And Anne Sharpe, someone new to Harrison, not only read and commented upon my Introduction and Notes, but tried them out on her upper and lower sixth formers. Her students at Malvern College proved sharp in their reading and frank in their criticism. Adam Carter, Hannah Denyer, Gavin Franklin, Nick Harrison, Lucy Jones, Dave Llewellyn, Josephine Melville-Smith, Will Middleton, Kate Moonie, Fran Roberts, David Rundle, Vikki Stevenson and Lee Worden are responsible for many improvements, not the least, the eradication of very many irritating parenthetical remarks!

I have watched enough theatre and done enough writing to know that Prospero is never in charge of the production even when it looks like he's centre stage. Somebody else, somewhere else is pulling a lot of strings. That is certainly true of *Permanently Bard*. Sophie Gordon Clark has been my *tireless* 'brave Ariel', making the magic happen (Prospero, I guess, knew as little about the technicalities of tempests as I do about computers); Cornelia Starks, my wise Gonzalo, ready with the books, the translations, the proofs; and Marie Hunt a kind of Caliban-without-the-grumbles, undertaking the domestic chores that bookish Prospero can't do without. As ever, my daughters, Bryony and Rowan, are my best spirits.

Prospero, of course, doesn't exist without the poet. Thank you, Tony, for the poems. And thank you Barrie Rutter for being an actor the poet wants to write for. It is because of you that I know Tony, and you, not I, are the real Prospero of his productions.

And every pound of this dead weight is pain
to Thomas Campey (Books) . . .

TONY   HARRISON

ONE

Heredity

How you became a poet's a mystery!
Wherever did you get your talent from?
I say: I had two uncles, Joe and Harry –
one was a stammerer, the other dumb.

Them & [uz]
(for Professors Richard Hoggart and Leon Cortez)

I

αἰαῖ , ay, ay !... stutterer Demosthenes
gob full of pebbles outshouting seas –

4 words only of *mi 'art aches* and... 'Mine's broken,
you barbarian, T.W.!' *He* was nicely spoken.
'Can't have our glorious heritage done to death!'

I played the Drunken Porter in *Macbeth*.

'Poetry's the speech of kings. You're one of those
Shakespeare gives the comic bits to: prose!
All poetry (even Cockney Keats?) you see
's been dubbed by [ʌs] into RP,
Received Pronunciation, please believe [ʌs]
your speech is in the hands of the Receivers.'

'We say [ʌs] not [uz], T.W.!' That shut my trap.
I doffed my flat a's (as in 'flat cap')
my mouth all stuffed with glottals, great
lumps to hawk up and spit out... *E-nun-ci-ate!*

II

So right, yer buggers, then! We'll occupy
your lousy leasehold Poetry.

I chewed up Littererchewer and spat the bones
into the lap of dozing Daniel Jones,
dropped the initials I'd been harried as
and used my name and own voice: [uz] [uz] [uz],
ended sentences with by, with, from,
and spoke the language that I spoke at home.
RIP RP, RIP T.W.
I'm *Tony* Harrison no longer you!

You can tell the Receivers where to go
(and not aspirate it) once you know
Wordsworth's *matter/water* are full rhymes,
[uz] can be loving as well as funny.

My first mention in the *Times*
automatically made Tony Anthony!

Thomas Campey and the Copernican System

The other day all thirty shillings' worth
of painfully collected waste was blown
off the heavy handcart high above the earth,
and scattered paper whirled around the town.

The earth turns round to face the sun in March,
he said, resigned, *it's bound to cause a breeze.*
Familiar last straws. His back's strained arch
questioned the stiff balance of his knees,

Thomas Campey, who, in each demolished home,
cherished a Gibbon with a gilt-worked spine,
Spengler and Mommsen, and a huge, black tome
with Latin titles for his own decline:

Tabes dorsalis; veins like flex, like fused
and knotted flex, with a cart on the cobbled road,
he drags for life old clothing, used
lectern bibles and cracked Copeland Spode,

Marie Corelli, Ouida and Hall Caine
and texts from Patience Strong in tortoise frames.
and every pound of this dead weight is pain
to Thomas Campey (Books) who often dreams

of angels in white crinolines all dressed
to kill, of God as Queen Victoria who grabs
him by the scruff and shoves his body pressed
quite straight again under St Anne's slabs.

And round Victoria Regina the Most High
swathed in luminous smokes like factories,
these angels serried in a dark, Leeds sky
chanting *Angina —a, Angina Pectoris.*

Keen winter is the worst time for his back,
squeezed lungs and damaged heart; just one
more sharp turn of the earth, those knees will crack
and he will turn his warped spine on the sun.

Leeds! Offer thanks to that Imperial Host,
squat on its thrones of Ormus and of Ind,
for bringing Thomas from his world of dust
to dust, and leisure of the simplest kind.

TWO

Me Tarzan

Outside the whistled gang-call, *Twelfth Street Rag*,
then a Tarzan yodel for the kid who's bored,
whose hand's on his liana... no, back
to Labienus and his flaming sword.

Off laikin', then to t'fish 'oil all the boys,
off tartin', off to t'flicks but on, on, on,
the foldaway card table, the green baize,
De Bello Gallico and lexicon.

It's only his jaw muscles that he's tensed
into an enraged *shit* that he can't go;
down with polysyllables, he's against
all pale-face Caesars, *for* Geronimo.

He shoves the frosted attic skylight, shouts:

Ah bloody can't ah've gorra Latin prose.

His bodiless head that's poking out 's
like patriarchal Cissy-bleeding-ro's.

Wordlists

There was only one more thing which had to be done,
a last message to leave behind on the last day of all:
and so he gathered up his strength in the midst of
a long stretch of silence and framed his lips to say
to me quite clearly the one word: Dictionary.

(*The Life of Joseph Wright*, 1885-1930)

I

Good parrots got good marks. I even got
a 100 in Divinity (posh schools' RI),
learned new long words and (wrongly stressed) *harlót*
I asked the meaning of so studiously.

I asked mi mam. She said she didn't know.
The Classics/RI master hummed and hawed.
(If only he'd've said it was a pro!)
New words: 'venery', 'VD' and 'bawd'!

Sometime... er... there's summat in that drawer...

photograph foetuses, a pinman with no prick,
things I learned out laiking years before
they serialised 'Life' in the *Sunday Pic*.

Words and wordlessness. Between the two
the gauge went almost ga-ga. No RI,
no polysyllables could see me through,
come glossolalia, duciloquy.

II

The *Funk & Wagnalls*? Does that still survive?
Uncle Harry most eloquent deaf-mute
jabbed at its lexis till it leaped to life
when there were Tory errors to confute.

A bible paper bomb that dictionary.
I learned to rifle through it at great speed.
He's dead. I've studied, got the OED
and other tongues I've slaved to speak or read:

I. & S dead Latin, L & S dead Greek,
one the now dead lexicographer gave me,
Ivan Poldauf, his English-Czech *slovník*;
Harrap's French 2 vols, a Swahili,
Cabrera's Afro-Cuban *Anagó*,
Hausa, Yoruba, both R.C. Abraham's

but not the tongue that once I used to know
but can't bone up on now, and that's mi mam's.

Breaking the Chain

The mams pig-sick of oilstains in the wash
wished for their sons a better class of gear,
'wear their own clothes into work' but not go posh,
go up a rung or two but settle near.

This meant the drawing office to the dads,
same place of work, but not blue-collar, white.
A box like a medal case went round the lads
as, one by one, their mams pushed them as 'bright'.

My dad bought it, from the last dad who still owed
the dad before, for a whole week's wage and drink.
I was brought down out of bed to have bestowed
the polished box wrapped in the *Sporting Pink*.

Looking at it now still breaks my heart!
The gap his gift acknowledged then 's as wide as
eternity, but I still can't bear to part
with these never passed on, never used, dividers.

Isolation

I cried once as a boy when I'd to leave her
at Christmas in the fourth year of the War,
taken to Killingbeck with scarlet fever,
but don't cry now, although I see once more
from the window of the York-Leeds diesel back
for her funeral, my place of quarantine,

and don't, though I notice by the same railtrack
hawthorns laden with red berries as they'd been
when we'd seen them the day that we returned
from the hospital on this same train together
and she taught me a county saying that she'd learned
as a child: *Berries bode bad winter weather!*

and don't, though the fresh grave's flecked with sleet,
and dad, with every fire back home switched on, 's
frozen,
     and don't,
           until I hear him bleat
round the ransacked house for his long johns.

Continuous

James Cagney was the one up both our streets.
His was the only art we ever shared.
A gangster film and choc ice were the treats
that showed about as much love as he dared.

He'd be my own age now in '49!
The hand that glinted with the ring he wore,
his father's, tipped the cold bar into mine
just as the organist dropped through the floor.

He's on the platform lowered out of sight
to organ music, this time on looped tape,
into a furnace with a blinding light
where only his father's ring will keep its shape.

I wear it now to Cagneys on my own
and sense my father's hands cupped round my treat –

they feel as though they've been chilled to the bone
from holding my ice cream all through *White Heat.*

Still

Tugging my forelock fathoming Xenophon
grimed Greek exams with grease and lost me marks,
so I whisper when the barber asks *Owt on?*
No, thank you! YES! Dad's voice behind me barks.

They made me wear dad's hair-oil to look 'smart'.
A parting scored the grease like some slash scar.
Such aspirations hair might have for ART
were lopped, and licked by dollops from his jar.

And if the page I'm writing on has smears
they're not the sort to lose me marks for mess
being self-examination's grudging tears
soaked into the blotter, Nothingness,
on seeing the first still I'd ever seen
of Rudolph Valentino, father, O
now, *now* I know why you used *Brilliantine*
to slick back your black hair so long ago.

An Old Score

Capless, conscious of the cold patch on my head
where my father's genes have made me almost bald
I walk along the street where he dropped dead,
my hair cut his length now, although I'm called
poet, in my passport.
                          When it touched my ears
he dubbed me *Paganinny* and it hurt.
I did then, and do now, choke back my tears –

Wi' 'air like that you ought to wear a skirt!

If I'd got a violin for every day
he'd said *weer's thi fiddle?* at my flowing hair
I'd have a whole string orchestra to play
romantic background as once more I'm there
where we went for my forced fortnightly clip
now under new, less shearing, ownership,
and in the end it's that that makes me cry –

JOE'S SALOON's become KURL UP & DYE!

A Good Read

That summer it was Ibsen, Marx and Gide.

I got one of his you-stuck-up-bugger looks:

ah sometimes think you read too many books.
ah nivver 'ad much time for a good read.

Good read! I bet! Your programme at United!
The labels on your whisky or your beer!
You'd never get unbearably excited
poring over Kafka or King Lear.

The only score you'd bother with 's your darts,
or fucking football...
                    (All this in my mind.)

I've come round to your position on 'the Arts'
but put it down in poems, that's the bind.

These poems about you, dad, should make good reads
for the bus you took from Beeston into town
for people with no time like you in Leeds –

once I'm writing I can't put you down!

Illuminations

I

The two machines on Blackpool's Central Pier,
The Long Drop and *The Haunted House* gave me
my thrills the holiday that post-war year
but my father watched me spend impatiently:

Another tanner's worth, but then no more!

But I sneaked back the moment that you napped.
50 weeks of ovens, and 6 years of war
made you want sleep and ozone, and you snapped:

Bugger the machines! Breathe God's fresh air!

I sulked all week, and wouldn't hold your hand.
I'd never heard you mention God, or swear,
and it took me until now to understand.

I see now all the piled old pence turned green,
enough to hang the murderer all year
and stare at millions of ghosts in the machine.

The penny dropped in time! Wish you were here!

II

We built and bombed Boche stalags on the sands,
and hunted for beached starfish on the rocks
and some days ended up all holding hands
gripping the pier machine that gave you shocks.
The current would connect. We'd feel the buzz
ravel our loosening ties to one tense grip,
the family circle, one continuous US!
That was the first year on my scholarship
and I'd be the one who'd make that circuit short.
I lectured them on neutrons and Ohm's law
and other half-baked Physics I'd been taught.
I'm sure my father felt I was a bore!

Two dead, but current still flows through us three
though the circle takes forever to complete –
eternity, annihilation, me,
that small bright charge of life where they both meet.

III *The Icing Hand*

That they lasted only till the next high tide
bothered me not him whose labour was to make
sugar lattices demolished when the bride,
with help from her groom's hot hand, first cut the cake.

His icing hand, gritty with sandgrains, guides
my pen when I try shaping memories of him
and his eyes scan with mine those rising tides
neither father nor his son could hope to swim.

His eyes stayed dry while I, the kid, would weep
to watch the castle that had taken us all day
to build and deck decay, one wave-surge sweep
our winkle-stuccoed edifice away.

Remembrance like iced cake crumbs in the throat,
remembrance like windblown Blackpool brine
overfills the poem's shallow moat
and first, ebbing, salts, then, flowing, floods this line.

IV

The family didn't always feel together.
Those silent teas with all of us apart
when no one spoke except about the weather
and not about his football or my art.

And in those silences the grating sound
of father's celery, the clock's loud tick,
the mine subsidence from deep underground
mi mam's loose bottom teeth's relentless click.

And when, I'm told, St James's came to fetch her,
My teeth! were the final words my mother said.
Being without them, even on a stretcher,
was more undignified than being dead.

Ay! I might have said, *and put her in her box
dressed in that long gown she bought to wear,
not to be outclassed by those posh frocks,
at her son's next New York première!*

Durham

St Cuthbert's shrine,
founded 999

(MNEMONIC)

ANARCHY and GROW YOUR OWN
whitewashed on to crumbling stone
fade in the drizzle. There's a man
handcuffed to warders in a black sedan.
A butcher dumps a sodden sack
of sheep pelts off his bloodied back,
then hangs the morning's killings out,
cup-cum-muzzle on each snout.

I've watched where this 'distinguished see'
takes off into infinity,
among transistor antennae,
and student smokers getting high,
and visiting Norwegian choirs
in raptures over Durham's spires,
lifers, rapists, thieves, ant-size
circle and circle at their exercise.

And Quasimodo's bird's-eye view
of big wigs and their retinue,
a five car Rolls Royce motorcade
of judgement draped in Town Hall braid,
I've watched the golden maces sweep
from courtrooms to the Castle keep
through winding Durham, the elect
before whom ids must genuflect.

But some stay standing and at one
God's irritating carillon
brings you to me; I feel like the hunch-
back taking you for lunch;
then bed. All afternoon two church-
high prison helicopters search
for escapees down by the Wear
and seem as though they're coming here.

Listen! Their choppers guillotine
all the enemies there've ever been
of Church and State, including me
for taking this small liberty.
Liberal, lover, communist,
Czechoslovakia, Cuba, grist,
grist for the power-driven mill
weltering in overkill.

And England? Quiet Durham? Threat
smokes off our lives like steam off wet
subsidences when summer rain
drenches the workings. You complain
that the machinery of sudden death,
Fascism, the hot bad breath
of Powers down small countries' necks
shouldn't interfere with sex.

They *are* sex, love, we must include
all these in love's beatitude.
Bad weather and the public mess
drive us to private tenderness,
though I wonder if together we,
alone two hours, can ever be
love's anti-bodies in the sick,
sick body politic.

At best we're medieval masons, skilled
but anonymous within our guild,
at worst defendants hooded in a car
charged with something sinister.
On the *status quo*'s huge edifice
we're just excrescences that kiss,
cathedral gargoyles that obtrude
their acts of 'moral turpitude'.

But turpitude still keeps me warm
in foul weather as I head for home
down New Elvet, through the town,
past the butcher closing down,

hearing the belfry jumble time
out over Durham. As I climb
rain blankets the pithills, mist
the chalkings of the anarchist.

I wait for the six-five Plymouth train
glowering at Durham. First rain,
then hail, like teeth spit from a skull,
then fog obliterate it. As we pull
out of the station through the dusk and fog,
there, lighting up, is Durham, dog
chasing its own cropped tail,
University, Cathedral, Gaol.

Book Ends

I

Baked the day she suddenly dropped dead
we chew it slowly that last apple pie.

Shocked into sleeplessness you're scared of bed.
We never could talk much, and now don't try.

You're like book ends, the pair of you, she'd say,
Hog that grate, say nothing, sit, sleep, stare...

The 'scholar' me, you, worn out on poor pay,
only our silence made us seem a pair.

Not as good for staring in, blue gas,
too regular each bud, each yellow spike.

At night you need my company to pass
and she not here to tell us we're alike!

Your life's all shattered into smithereens.

Back in our silences and sullen looks,
for all the Scotch we drink, what's still between 's
not the thirty or so years, but books, books, books.

II

The stone's too full. The wording must be terse.
There's scarcely room to carve the FLORENCE on it –

*Come on, it's not as if we're wanting verse.
It's not as if we're wanting a whole sonnet!*

After tumblers of neat *Johnny Walker*
(I think that both of us we're on our third)
you said you'd always been a clumsy talker
and couldn't find another, shorter word
for 'beloved' or for 'wife' in the inscription,
but not too clumsy that you still can't cut:

You're supposed to be the bright boy at description
and you can't tell them what the fuck to put!

I've got to find the right words on my own.

I've got the envelope that he'd been scrawling,
mis-spelt, mawkish, stylistically appalling
but I can't squeeze more love into their stone.

Blocks

A droning vicar bores the congregation
and misquotes *Ecclesiastes* Chapter 3.
If anyone should deliver an oration
it should be me, her son, in poetry.

All the family round me start to sob.
For all my years of Latin and of Greek
they'd never seen the point of 'for a job',
I'm not prepared to stand up now and speak.

A time to... plough back into the soil
the simple rhymes that started at her knee,
the poetry, that 'sedentary toil'
that began, when her lap was warm, with ABC.

Blocks with letters. Lettered block of stone.
I have to move the blocks to say farewell.

I hear the family cry, the vicar drone
and VALE, MATER 's all that I can spell.

Bringing Up

It was a library copy otherwise
you'd've flung it in the fire in disgust.
Even cremation can't have dried the eyes
that wept for weeks about my 'sordid lust'.

The undertaker would have thought me odd
or I'd have put my book in your stiff hand.
You'd have been embarrassed though to meet your God
clutching those poems of mine that you'd like banned.

I thought you could hold my *Loiners*, and both burn!

And there together in the well wrought urn,
what's left of you, the poems of your child,
devoured by one flame, unreconciled,
like soots on washing, black on bone-ash white.

Maybe you see them in a better light!

But I still see you weeping, your hurt looks:

You weren't brought up to write such mucky books!

Long Distance

I

Your bed's got two wrong sides. Your life's all grouse.
I let your phone-call take its dismal course:

Ah can't stand it no more, this empty house!

Carrot's choke us wi'out your mam's white sauce!

*Them sweets you brought me, you can have 'em back.
Ah'm diabetic now. Got all the facts.*

(The diabetes comes hard on the track
of two coronaries and cataracts.)

Ah've allus liked things sweet! But now ah push
food down mi throat! Ah'd sooner do wi'out.
And t'only reason now for beer 's to flush
(so t'dietician said) mi kidneys out.

When I come round, they'll be laid out, the sweets,
Lifesavers, my father's New World treats,
still in the big brown bag, and only bought
rushing through JFK as a last thought.

II

Though my mother was already two years dead
Dad kept her slippers warming by the gas,
put hot water bottles her side of the bed
and still went to renew her transport pass.

You couldn't just drop in. You had to phone.
He'd put you off an hour to give him time
to clear away her things and look alone
as though his still raw love were such a crime.

He couldn't risk my blight of disbelief
though sure that very soon he'd hear her key
scrape in the rusted lock and end his grief.
He *knew* she'd just popped out to get the tea.

I believe that life ends with death, and that is all.
You haven't both gone shopping; just the same,
in my new black leather phone book there's your name
and the disconnected number I still call.

Timer

Gold survives the fire that's hot enough
to make you ashes in a standard urn.
An envelope of coarse official buff
contains your wedding ring which wouldn't burn.

Dad told me I'd to tell them at St James's
that the ring should go in the incinerator.
That 'eternity' inscribed with both their names is
his surety that they'd be together, 'later'.

I signed for the parcelled clothing as the son,
the cardy, apron, pants, bra, dress –

The clerk phoned down: *6-8-8-3-1?*
Has she still her ring on? (Slight pause) *Yes!*

It's on my warm palm now, your burnished ring!

I feel your ashes, head, arms, breasts, womb, legs,
sift through its circle slowly, like that thing
you used to let me watch to time the eggs.

Turns

I thought it made me look more 'working class'
(as if a bit of chequered cloth could bridge that gap!)
I did a turn in it before the glass.
My mother said: *It suits you, your dad's cap.*
(She preferred me to wear suits and part my hair:
You're every bit as good as that lot are!)

All the pension queue came out to stare.
Dad was sprawled beside the postbox (still VR),
his cap turned inside up beside his head,
smudged H A H in purple Indian ink
and Brylcreem slicks displayed so folk might think
he wanted charity for dropping dead.

He never begged. For nowt! Death's reticence
crowns his life's, and *me*, I'm opening my trap
to busk the class that broke him for the pence
that splash like brackish tears into our cap.

Next Door

I

Ethel Jowett died still hoping not to miss
next year's *Mikado* by the D'Oyly Carte.
For being her 'male escort' (9!) to this
she gave my library its auspicious start:

The Kipling Treasury. My name. The date:
Tony Harrison   1946
in dip-in-penmanship type copperplate
with proper emphasis on thins and thicks.

Mi mam was 'that surprised' how many came
to see the cortège off and doff their hats –
All the 'old lot' left gave her the same
bussing back from 'Homes' and Old Folk's Flats.

Since mi mam dropped dead mi dad's took fright.

His dicky ticker beats its quick retreat:

It won't be long before Ah'm t'only white!

Or t'Town Hall's thick red line sweeps through t'whole street.

IV

All turbans round here now, forget flat caps!

They've taken over everything bar t'CO-OP.
Pork's gone west, chitt'lins, trotters, dripping baps!
And booze an' all, if it's a Moslem owns t'new shop.

Ay, t'Off Licence, *that's gone Paki in t'same way!*
(You took your jug and bought your bitter draught)
Ah can't get over it, mi dad'll say,
smelling curry in a pop shop. Seems all daft.

Next door but one this side 's front room wi t'
Singers hell for leather all day long 's
some sort o' sweatshop bi the looks on it
running up them dresses... them... sarongs!

Last of the 'old lot' still left in your block.
Those times, they're gone. The 'old lot' can't come back.

Both doors I notice now you double lock –

he's already in your shoes, your next-door black.

Marked with D.

When the chilled dough of his flesh went in an oven
not unlike those he fuelled all his life,
I thought of his cataracts ablaze with Heaven
and radiant with the sight of his dead wife,
light streaming from his mouth to shape her name,
'not Florence and not Flo but always Florrie'.
I thought how his cold tongue burst into flame
but only literally, which makes me sorry,
sorry for his sake there's no Heaven to reach.
I get it all from Earth my daily bread
but he hungered for release from mortal speech
that kept him down, the tongue that weighed like lead.

The baker's man that no one will see rise
and England made to feel like some dull oaf
is smoke, enough to sting one person's eyes
and ash (not unlike flour) for one small loaf.

Punchline

No! Revolution never crossed your mind!
For the kids who never made it through the schools
the Northern working class escaped the grind
as boxers or comedians, or won the pools.

Not lucky, no physique, too shy to joke,
you scraped together almost 3 weeks' pay
to buy a cast-off uke that left you broke.
You mastered only two chords, G and A!

That's why when I've heard George Formby that I've wept.
I'd always wondered what the thing was for,
I now know was a plectrum, that you'd kept,
but kept hidden, in your secret condom drawer.

The day of your cremation which I missed
I saw an old man strum a uke he'll never play,
cap spattered with tossed dimes. I made a fist
round my small change, your son, and looked away.

Background Material

My writing desk. Two photos, mam and dad.
A birthday, him. Their ruby wedding, her.
Neither one a couple and both bad.
I make out what's behind them from the blur.

Dad's in our favourite pub, now gone for good.
My father and his background are both gone,
but hers has my Welsh cottage and a wood
that still shows those same greens eight summers on,
though only the greenness of it 's stayed the same.

Though one of them 's in colour and one 's not,
the two are joined, apart from their shared frame,
by what, for photographers, would mar each shot:

in his, if you look close, the gleam, the light,
me in his blind right eye, but minute size –

in hers, as though just cast from where I write,
a shadow holding something to its eyes.

Fire-eater

My father speaking was like conjurers I'd seen
pulling bright silk hankies, scarves, a flag
up out of their innards, red, blue, green,
so many colours it would make me gag.

Dad's eldest brother had a shocking stammer.
Dad punctuated sentence ends with but...
Coarser stuff than silk they hauled up grammar
knotted together deep down in their gut.

Theirs are the acts I nerve myself to follow.
I'm the clown sent in to clear the ring.
Theirs are the tongues of fire I'm forced to swallow
then bring back knotted, one continuous string
igniting long-pent silences, and going back
to Adam fumbling with Creation's names,
and though my vocal chords get scorched and black
there'll be a constant singing from the flames.

Lines to My Grandfathers

I

Ploughed parallel as print the stony earth.
The straight stone walls defy the steep grey slopes.
The place's rightness for my mother's birth
exceeds the pilgrim grandson's wildest hopes –

Wilkinson farmed Thrang Crag, Martindale.

Horner was the Haworth signalman.

Harrison kept a pub with home-brewed ale:

fell farmer, railwayman, and *publican*,

and he, while granma slaved to tend the vat
graced the rival bars 'to make comparisons',
Queen's Arms, the Duke of this, the Duke of that,
while his was known as just 'The Harrisons''.

He carried cane and *guineas,* no coin baser!
He dressed the gentleman beyond his place
and paid in gold for beer and whisky chaser
but took his knuckleduster, 'just in case'.

II

The one who lived with us was grampa Horner
who, I remember, when a sewer rat
got driven into our dark cellar corner
booted it to pulp and squashed it flat.

He cobbled all our boots. I've got his last.
We use it as a doorstop on warm days.
My present is propped open by their past
and looks out over straight and narrow ways:

the way one ploughed his land, one squashed a rat,
kept railtracks clear, or, dressed up to the nines,
with waxed moustache, gold chain, his cane, his hat,
drunk as a lord could foot it on straight lines.

Fell farmer, railwayman and publican,
I strive to keep my lines direct and straight,
and try to make connections where I can –

the knuckleduster's now my paperweight!

Self Justification

Me a poet! My daughter with maimed limb
became a more than tolerable sprinter.
And Uncle Joe. Impediment spurred him,
the worst stammerer I've known, to be a printer.

He handset type much faster than he spoke.
Those cruel consonants, *m*s, *p*s and *b*s
on which his jaws and spirit almost broke
flicked into order with sadistic ease.

It seems right that Uncle Joe, 'b-buckshee
from the works', supplied those scribble pads
on which I stammered my first poetry
that made me seem a cissy to the lads.

Their aggro towards me, my need of them 's
what keeps my would-be mobile tongue still tied –
aggression, struggle, loss, blank printer's ems
by which all   eloquence   gets justified.

THREE

Classics Society
(Leeds Grammar School 1552-1952)

The grace of Tullies eloquence doth excell
any Englishmans tongue... my barbarous stile...

The tongue our leaders use to cast their spell
was once denounced as 'rude', 'gross', 'base' and 'vile'.

How fortunate we are who've come so far!

We boys can take old Hansards and translate
the British Empire into SPQR
but nothing demotic or too up-to-date,
and not the English that I speak at home,
not Hansard standards, and if Antoninus
spoke like delinquent Latin back in Rome
he'd probably get gamma double minus.

And so the lad who gets the alphas works
the hardest in his class at his translation
and finds good Ciceronian for Burke's:

a dreadful schism in the British nation.

National Trust

Bottomless pits. There's one in Castleton,
and stout upholders of our law and order
one day thought its depth worth wagering on
and borrowed a convict hush-hush from his warder
and winched him down; and back, flayed, grey, mad, dumb.

Not even a good flogging made him holler!

O gentlemen, a better way to plumb
the depths of Britain 's dangling a scholar,
say, here at the booming shaft at Towanroath,
now National Trust, a place where they got tin,
those gentlemen who silenced the men's oath
and killed the language that they swore it in.

The dumb go down in history and disappear
and not one gentleman 's been brought to book:

Mes den hep tavas a-gollas y dyr

(Cornish)
       'the tongueless man gets his land took.'

The Rhubarbarians

I

Those glottals glugged like poured pop, each
rebarbative syllable, remembrancer, raise
'mob' *rhubarb-rhubarb* to a tribune's speech
crossing the crackle as the hayricks blaze.

The gaffers' blackleg Boswells at their side.
Horsfall of Ottiwells, if the bugger could,
'd've liked to (exact words recorded) *ride
up to my saddle-girths in Luddite blood.*

What t'mob said to the cannons on the mills,
shouted to soldier, scab and sentinel
's silence, parries and hush on whistling hills,
shadows in moonlight playing knurr and spell.

It wasn't poetry, though. Nay, wiseowl Leeds
pro rege et lege schools, nobody needs
your drills and chanting to parrot right
the *tusky-tusky* of the pikes that night.

II

*(on translating Smetana's Prodaná Nevěsta for
the Metropolitan Opera, New York)*

> One afternoon the Band Conductor up on his stand
> Somehow lost his baton it flew out of his hand
> So I jumped in his place and conducted the band
> With mi little stick of Blackpool Rock!
>
> GEORGE FORMBY

Finale of ACT II. Though I resist
blurring the clarity of *hanba* (shame)
not wanting the least nuance to be missed
syllables run to rhubarb just the same...

Sorry, dad, you won't get that quatrain
(I'd like to be the poet my father reads!)
It's all from you once saying on the train
how most of England's rhubarb came from Leeds.

Crotchets and quavers, rhubarb silhouettes,
dark-shy sea-horse heads through waves of dung!
Rhubarb arias, duets, quartets
soar to precision from our common tongue.

The uke in the attic manhole once was yours!

Watch me on the rostrum wave my arms –

mi little stick of Leeds-grown *tusky* draws
galas of rhubarb from the MET-set palms.

Divisions

I

All aggro in tight clothes and skinhead crops
they think that like themselves I'm on the dole.
Once in the baths that mask of 'manhood' drops.
Their decorated skins lay bare a soul.

Teenage dole-wallah piss-up, then tattoos.
Brown Ale and boys' bravado numbs their fright –
MOTHER in ivy, blood reds and true blues
against that North East skin so sunless white.

When next he sees United lose a match,
his bovvers on, his scarf tied round his wrist,
his rash NEWCASTLE RULES will start to scratch,
he'll aerosol the walls, then go get pissed...

So I hope the TRUE LOVE on your arm stays true,
the MOTHER on your chest stays loved, not hated.

But most I hope for jobs for all of you –

next year your tattooed team gets relegated!

II

Wartime bunkers, runways overgrown,
streets named for the town's two England caps;
cricket played with shovelblade and stone,
the daylight's rotten props near to collapse.

HEALTH (H changed to W) FOR ALL
with its *Never Have Another Haemorrhoid*
is all that decorates the tap-room wall
of this pub for pensioners and unemployed.

The Brewery that owns this place supports
only the unambiguously 'male'
Northern working class spectator sports
that suit the image of its butch *Brown Ale*,
that puts hair on your chest, and makes you fight,
and when you're legless makes a man of you!

The *Brown Ale* drinkers watch me as I write:

one front door orange in a row all blue!

Y

I'm good with curtains

MRS THATCHER

The thing I drink
from above the earth
's by *Technoplastics Inc.*
(Fort Worth)

I hear the chinks
of pukka glass
from what I think 's
called Business Class,

my taste buds impressed
as bustle helps waft
the Premium repast
to the Y class aft.

Farther fore there's china
and choices for dinner.
The wines get finer,
the glass thinner.

Veuve Cliquot for the man
with a 1st thirst; for me
a tiny ring-pull can
of California Chablis!

From our plastic drinking,
O Ys of all nations,
it's maybe worth thinking
that the one consolation 's:

if the engines fail
and we go into a dive
only Ys in the tail
ever seem to survive!

As the stewardesses serve
first to 1st, last to Y,
I can't fail to observe,
as on earth so in the sky,

that the U.S.A.
draws no drapes –
the First Class can pay
while the Y Class gapes –

pour encourager...
any man can fly
Premium if he can pay
(or his company).

We curtain the classes
while they eat,
the plastics from glasses,
we are so discreet!

And from LHR to JFK
from JFK to LHR
things are going to stay
just as they are.

Summoned by Bells

The art of letters will come to an end before A.D. 2000...
I shall survive as a curiosity.

EZRA POUND

O Zeppelins! O Zeppelins!
prayed poet E.P.
any Boche gets 60 pence
to bust this campanolatry!

Doubles, triples, caters, cinques
for corpse or Christmas joys
for him, or anyone who thinks,
may be 'foul nuisance' and mere noise.

Carillons can interfere
and ruin concentration.
I've had it wrecked, my rhythmic ear,
by the new faith of the nation.

So sympathise with E.P.'s plight.
This moment now it's hard to hold
this rhythm in my head and write
while those bloody bells are tolled.

St Mary Abbot's, they're passé.
What gets into my skull
any time of night or day
are the new bells of John Bull,

The new calls to the nation:
Securi-curi-curi-cor!
Join the fight against inflation!
Double-Chubb your door!

'Beat Inflation' adverts call.
Invest in stronger locks!
Display for all on your front wall
the crime-deterrent box.

Almost every day one goes
and the new faith that it rings
is vested in new videos
and the sacredness of things.

I got done once. No piercing peal
alerted neighbourhood or force
but then there's nothing here to steal
bar 'a few battered books', of course.

The poor sneak thief, all he could do
he had so little time to act,
was grab a meagre coin or two
and my bag there ready packed.

What bothers me perhaps the most
is I never heard the thief,
being obsessively engrossed
in rhymes of social grief.

In haste behind the garden wall
he unzipped my bag. Bad luck!
One glance told him that his haul
was 50 copies of one book!

Poems! Poems! All by me!
He dropped the lot and ran
(and who would buy hot poetry
from a poor illiterate man?)

deeply pissed by what he'd found,
dumped books and bag unzipped.
He'd've even ditched an Ezra Pound
Cantos manuscript.

I got my books, he went scot-free,
no summons, gaol or fines.
I used him for such poetry
this alarm leaves in these lines

on 'a botched civilisation'
E.P. helped to rebotch
where bells toll for a nation
that's one great Neighbourhood Watch.

Art & Extinction

*When I hear of the destruction of a species I feel as if
all the works of some great writer had perished.*

THEODORE ROOSEVELT, 1899

1 *The Birds of America*

(i) JOHN JAMES AUDUBON (1785-1851)

The struggle to preserve once spoken words
from already too well-stuffed taxonomies
is a bit like Audubon's when painting birds,
whose method an admirer said was this:
Kill 'em, wire 'em, paint 'em, kill a fresh 'un!

The plumage even of the brightest faded.
The artist had to shoot in quick succession
till all the feathers were correctly shaded.

Birds don't pose for pictures when alive!
Audubon's idea of restraint,
doing the Pelican, was 25
dead specimens a day for *one* in paint.

By using them do we save words or not?

As much as Audubon's art could save a,
say, godwit, or a grackle, which he shot
and then saw 'multiplied by Havell's graver'.

Among death-protected creatures in a case,
'The Earth's Endangered Species' on display
at a jam-packed terminal at JFK,
killing time again, I see my face
with Hawksbill Turtle, scrimshawed spermwhale bone,
the Margay of the family *Felidae*,
that, being threatened, cost the earth to buy.

And now with scientists about to clone
the long-haired mammoth back from Soviet frost,
my reflection's on the species the World's lost,
or will be losing in a little while,
which, as they near extinction, grow in worth,
the leopard, here a bag and matching purse,
the dancing shoes that were Nile crocodile,

the last *Felis Pardalis* left on Earth,

the poet preserved beneath deep permaverse.

5 *Dark Times*

That the *Peppered Moth* was white and now is dark 's
a lesson in survival for Mankind.

Around the time Charles Darwin had declined
the dedication of *Das Kapital* by Marx
its predators could spot it on the soot
but Industrial Revolution and Evolution taught
the moth to black its wings and not get caught
where all of Nature perished, or all but.

When lichens lighten some old smoke-grimed trees
and such as Yorkshire's millstacks now don't burn
and fish nose waters stagnant centuries,
can *Biston Carbonaria* relearn,

if Man's awakened consciousness succeeds
in turning all these tides of blackness back
and diminishing the need for looking black,

to flutter white again above new Leeds?

The Lords of Life

The snake our cracker neighbour had to scotch
was black and white and beautiful to watch.
I'd watch it shift its length, stay still, sashay,
shunting its flesh on shuffled vertebrae
for days before, and thought of it as 'mine'
so long had I wondered at its pliant spine.
My neighbour thinks it queer my sense of loss.
He took a branch festooned with Spanish moss,
at the cooler end of one long afternoon,
and pestled my oaksnake's head into a spoon
he flourished laughing at his dogs, then slung
the slack ladle of its life to where it hung
snagged on a branch for buzzards till, stripped bare,
it trailed like a Chinese kite-string in the air.
Waal! he exclaimed, *if ahda knowed you guys*
liked *snakes on your land…* he turns and sighs
at such greenhornery. I'd half a mind
to say I'd checked the snake's a harmless kind
in *two* encyclopaedias but know the looks
I'd get from him for 'talking books'. –
There's something fairy (I can hear him say)
about a guy that watches snakes all goddam day!
The wife he bullies says: *O Bill, let be!*
There's doers and there's watchers, maybe he…
Ain't no doer, says he, that's plain to see!
I seed him sit out on their porch and read
some goddam great Encyclopaed-
ia, yeah, read! *What does the fairy DO?*
O Bill! she says, *not everyone's like you.*
And you'd be the first man to stand up and say
that people living in the USA
have every right to live the way they please. –
Yeah! But those guys look too young for retirees!
Nothing that I did made any sense
but I think he offered me as recompense
for battering my snake the chance to see
the alligators on his property.

Each Sunday his riding mower wouldn't stop
till every blade of grass had had its crop,
so that the bald, burned earth showed through the green
but any snake that trespassed was soon seen.
That was the front, but out there in the back
he hadn't even hacked a proper track
down to the swampy lake, his own retreat
kept as wild as the front part was kept neat.
This was his wilderness, his very own
left just as it was, rank, overgrown,
and into this he went with guns and beer
to wallow in his dreams of the frontier
and shoot the gators we were seeing glide
with egrets on their backs from side to side.
The egrets ride in threes their gator skiffs,
Pharaohs' sarcophagi with hieroglyphs!
He offered me his rifle: *Wanna try?*
Go for the big ones, not the smaller fry!
They've taken gators off the Endangered List.
I took aim and, deliberately, missed.
He blasted three egrets like a fairground shy
and then the gator they were ferried by.
Then we sat down at his fire and watched the day,
now reddened at the edges, drain away.
The hissing of damp logs and ringpull Bud
drunk from the can, his seal of brotherhood
(the sort where I'd play Abel and him Cain!)
I can't stand his beer but don't complain
as he flings them across the fire for me to catch:
round 1: the shooting. 2: the boozing match!
Each dead can he crushed flat and tossed aside.
(When I was safe back home I also tried
and found, to my great chagrin, aluminum
crushable with pressure from one thumb!)
We stare into his cookout and exchange
neighbourly nothings, gators still in range.
Liberal with his beer-cans he provokes
his gator-watching guest with racist jokes.
Did you know, sir, that gators only eat
dogs and niggers, darker sorts of meat?
But you can eat him if he won't eat you.
I'll give you a gator steak to barbecue.

(He knew that cooking's something that I *do*!)
He'd watched me cooking, and, done out of doors,
cooking could be classed among male chores.
His suspicions of me as an idle loafer
who couldn't gut a mullet or stew gopher
I tried, when I felt him watching, to dispel
by letting him see me working, working well.
I make sure, when he stares over, my swing's true
when I heave the axe like I've seen rednecks do,
both hands well-balanced on the slippery haft,
or make certain that he sees me when I waft
the coals to a fierce glow with my straw hat,
the grill bars spitting goat or gator fat.
If them fireants ain't stopped with gasoline
you can say goodbye to every inch of green.
They say on the TV they'll eat their way,
if we don't check 'em, through the USA!
The 'red peril' 's what we call them bugs down here.
(A hiss for those villains from his seventh beer!)
From this house, you know, we're near enough to see
space launchings live. The wife watched on TV,
then dashed outside, and saw, with her own eyes,
'like a silver pen', she said, 'The Enterprise',
then rushed back for the message from the Prez
who'd just been wounded by some nut. He says:
We feel like giants again! *Taking over space*
has made Goliaths of the human race.
Me, I was in the rowboat, trying to relax.
I'd gotten me some chicken, 2 or 3 6-packs
like relaxing, and I zoomed out of a snooze
with a sudden start, the way you do with booze,
and saw our spaceship, clear as I see you,
like a bullet disappearing in the blue.
I must say that it made me mighty proud.
I sang God Bless America *out loud*
to those goddam alligators then I got
the biggest of the brutes with one sharp shot.
(But a man might get, say, lovesick, then she shoots
not one of your unendangered gator brutes
that glide so gracefully through silver ooze
and gladden gourmets in those Cross Creek stews,
and instead of potting dumb beasts like your gators

shoots the most acknowledged of all legislators,
on whose scaled back as corpse and cortège glide
the egret of the soul bums its last ride!)
Stuck goat fat's spitting from my still hot grill.
I've eaten very well, and drunk my fill,
and sip my *Early Times*, and to and fro
rock in the rocker watching ashes blow
off the white-haired charcoals and away
into the darkness of the USA.
Higher than the fireflies, not as high as stars,
the sparks fly up between the red-hot bars.
I want no truck myself with outer space
except to gaze on from some earthly place
very much like this one in the South,
the taste of *Early Times* warm in my mouth.
Popping meals in pills in zero G
's not the dining that would do for me.
I'm feeling too composed to break the spell
when mosquitoes probe the veins of mine that swell
like blue earthworms. A head with sting
burrows in the blue, starts syphoning.
Let be! the watcher in me says, *Let be!*
but suddenly the doer side of me
(though my cracker neighbour couldn't, though he'd tried,
fathom if I'd got a doer side!)
swats the bastard and its legs like hair
sprout from my drop of blood on the cane chair.
The day's heat rolls away to make night thunder.
I look at the clouded planets and I wonder
if the God who blessed America's keen eye,
when He looked on that launching, chanced to spy,
in this shrinking world with far too many men,
either the cock-pecked wife who saw a pen…
(if I'd seen it going I'd've said
it was my snake sprayed silver, whose black head
my neighbour battered concave like a spoon,
pointing its harmless nose towards the moon,
lacquered in rigor mortis and not bent
into eternity's encirclement,
curled in a circle, sucking its own tail,
the formed continuum of female/male,
time that devours and endlessly renews,

time the open maw and what it chews,
the way it had mine chewed down here on earth,
the emblem of continuous rebirth
a bleached spine like one strand of Spanish moss –
for all above *vide sub* Ouroboros!
All this is booktalk, buddy, mere En-
cyclopaedia know-how, not for men!)...

either the cock-pecked wife who saw a pen,
or the lurching rowboat where a red-faced man's
sprawled beside his shotgun and crushed cans,
who saw a bullet streak off on its trek,
and to that watching God was a mere speck,
the human mite, his rowboat lapped with blood,
the giant gator hunter killing BUD!

FOUR

Sonnets for August 1945

1 *The Morning After*

I.

The fire left to itself might smoulder weeks.
Phone cables melt. Paint peels from off back gates.
Kitchen windows crack; the whole street reeks
of horsehair blazing. Still, it celebrates.

Though people weep, their tears dry from the heat.
Faces flushed with flame, beer, sheer relief
and such a sense of celebration in our street
for me it still means joy though banked with grief.

And that, now clouded, sense of public joy
with war-worn adults wild in their loud fling
has never come again since as a boy
I saw Leeds people dance and heard them sing.

There's still that dark, scorched circle on the road.
The morning after kids like me helped spray
hissing upholstery spring wire that still glowed
and cobbles boiling with black gas tar for VJ.

II.

The Rising Sun was blackened on those flames.
The jabbering tongues of fire consumed its rays.
Hiroshima, Nagasaki were mere names
for us small boys who gloried in our blaze.

The blood-red ball, first burnt to blackout shreds,
took hovering batwing on the bonfire's heat
above the *Rule Britannias* and the bobbing heads
of the VJ hokey-cokey in our street.

The kitchen blackout cloth became a cloak
for me to play at fiend Count Dracula in.
I swirled it near the fire. It filled with smoke.
Heinz ketchup dribbled down my vampire's chin.

That circle of scorched cobbles scarred with tar 's
a night sky globe nerve-rackingly all black,
both hemispheres entire but with no stars,
an Archerless zilch, a Scaleless zodiac.

Initial Illumination

Farne cormorants with catches in their beaks
shower fishscale confetti on the shining sea.
The first bright weather here for many weeks
for my Sunday G-day train bound for Dundee,
off to St Andrew's to record a reading,
doubtful, in these dark days, what poems can do,
and watching the mists round Lindisfarne receding
my doubt extends to Dark Age Good Book too.
Eadfrith the Saxon scribe/illuminator
incorporated cormorants I'm seeing fly
round the same island thirteen centuries later
into the *In principio*'s initial I.
Billfrith's begemmed and jewelled boards got looted
by raiders gung-ho for booty and berserk,
the sort of soldiery that's still recruited
to do today's dictators' dirty work,
but the initials in St John and in St Mark
graced with local cormorants in ages,
we of a darker still keep calling Dark,
survive in those illuminated pages.
The word of God so beautifully scripted
by Eadfrith and Billfrith the anchorite
Pentagon conners have once again conscripted
to gloss the cross on the precision sight.
Candlepower, steady hand, gold leaf, a brush
were all that Eadfrith had to beautify
the word of God much bandied by George Bush
whose word illuminated midnight sky
and confused the Baghdad cock who was betrayed
by bombs into believing the day was dawning
and crowed his heart out at the deadly raid
and didn't live to greet the proper morning.

Now with the noonday headlights in Kuwait
and the burial of the blackened in Baghdad
let them remember, all those who celebrate,
that their good news is someone else's bad
or the light will never dawn on poor Mankind.
Is it open-armed at all that victory V,

that insular initial intertwined
with slack-necked cormorants from black laquered sea,
with trumpets bulled and bellicose and blowing
for what men claim as victories in their wars,
with the fire-hailing cock and all those crowing
who don't yet smell the dunghill at their claws?

FROM **Agamemnon,**
the first play in **The Oresteia**

Enter CHORUS.

CHORUS.
Ten years since clanchief Menelaus
and his bloodkin Agamemnon
(the twin-yoked rule from clan-chief Atreus –
double thronestones, double chief-staves)
pursued the war-suit against Priam,
launched the 1000 ship armada
off from Argos to smash Troy.

Mewing warcries   preybirds   shrilling
nest-theft   childloss   wild frustration
nestling snaffled   preybirds soaring
wildly sculling   swirling airstreams
using broad birdwings like oars
birthpangs   nothing   nestcare   nothing
nothing   fostered nestlings   nothing
crying   mewing   preybirds   shrilling

But one of the god powers up above them –
Apollo   Pan   or Zeus high he-god
hearing the birds' shrill desolation,
birds, guest-strangers in god-spaces
sends down the slow but certain Fury
to appease the grudge the grieved birds feel

So Zeus protector of man's guestright
sends the avenging sons of Atreus
down on Paris son of Priam
because of Helen, lust-lode, man-hive,
Helen the she manned by too many hes.

Bedbond   no   not bedbond   spearclash
swordhafts shattered   hacked bones smashed
sparring   skirmish   dustclouds   bloodstorm
Trojans   Greeks   not bedbond   bloodbath

The war in Troy's still in a stalemate
marking time at where it's got to
till the fulfilment that's been fated.
Once the Fury's after victims
no sacrifices   no libations
stop the headlong grudge's onrush.

But as for us   recruiter's refuse,
too old to join the expedition,
shrivelled leafage left to wither,
we go doddering about on sticks.
Neither the nurseling nor the senile
have juice enough to serve the Wargod.
Wargod-fodder's prime manhood.

Argos geezers, back to bairnhood,
ghosts still walking after cockcrow,
old men, dreams abroad in daylight.

She-child of Tyndareos, Clytemnestra,
what news have you had, what fresh reports?
You've given orders for sacrifice. Why?

All the godstones of this bloodclan
earthgods   skygods   threshold   market
look   they're all alight   all blazing

Look here   and there   the flaring firebrands
coaxed into flame by smooth-tongued torch-oils
brought out of store for great occasions

If you can tell us give us some comfort
soothe all that grief that's chewed into our guts.
Hope glimmers a little in these lit godstones,
blunts the sharp chops of gnashing despair.

Gab's the last god-gift of the flabby and feeble –
singing the omens that mobilised Argos:

Two preybirds came as prophecy
blackwing and silverhue
came for our twin kings to see
out of the blue   the blue

The right side was the side they flew
spear side   luck side   War
one blackwing   one silverhue
and everybody saw

and everybody saw them tear
with talon and with claw
the belly of a pregnant hare
and everybody saw

and everybody saw the brood
from their mauled mother torn
wallowing in warm lifeblood
and dead as soon as born

blackwing and silverhue
prophesying War
the twin preybirds that cry and mew
hungering for more...

Batter, batter the doom-drum, but believe there'll be better!

Calchas the clanseer cunning in seercraft
when he saw before him the armed sons of Atreus
knew what menfolk were meant by the preybirds –
Agamemnon   Menelaus   battle-hungry hare-devourers...

'Hosts commanded by twin birds
soldiers who leave these shores
first Fate will waste Troy's crops and herds
then make the inner city yours

The moment when the iron bit
's between the jaws of Troy
may no skycurse glower down on it
and no godgrudge destroy

Artemis   pure she-god   stung
with pity for the hare
all mothers and their unborn young
come under her kind care

her father's hounds with silent wings
swoop down on that scared beast
Artemis   she loves wee things
and loathes the preybirds' feast.'

blackwing and silverhue
prophesying War
the twin preybirds that cry and mew
hungering for more...

Batter, batter the doom-drum, but believe there'll be better!

Artemis pure she-god   stung
with pity for the hare
all mothers and their unborn young
come under her kind care

Kind even to the lion-pup
you're the one we cry to, you!
Kind to wild beasts at the pap
stop bad signs coming true.

Apollo   he-god   healer   your she-kin
Artemis   intervene   prevent her
sending winds on the fleet from the wrong direction
keeping the armada too long at anchor,

making a blood-debt sacrifice certain,
a sacrifice no one wants to eat meat from,
a sacrifice no one wants to sing songs to,
whetting the grudge in the clanchief's household,
weakening the bond between woman and manlord,
a grudge wanting blood for the spilling of childblood,
a grudge brooding only on seizing its blood-dues.

These omens both fair and foreboding
Calchas the clanseer saw in the birdsigns –

Batter, batter the doom-drum, but believe there'll be better!

So Agamemnon first clanchief of Argos
found no fault in the clanseer's foretelling
and went where the winds of his life-lot were listing,
the Achaian armada still anchored off Aulis.

Wind-force and wave-swell   keep the ships shorebound
men sapped of spirit   supplies running short
foodpots and grain jars   crapping their contents
ship planks gape open   frayed cables and rigging
time dragging   each day seeming two days
the flower of Argos   bedraggled and drooping

Calchas the clanseer   saw into the storm-cause –
Artemis   she-god   goaded to godgrudge

The clans and the clanchiefs   clamour for sea calm
The god-sop that gets it   makes their guts sicken
The cure for the stormblast   makes strong men craven

The clanchiefs of Argos   drummed their staves on the earth
and wept and wept   and couldn't stop weeping

Then the first he-child of Atreus   Agamemnon
choked back his crying   and finally spoke:

hard   hard for a general   not to obey
hard   hard for a father   to kill his girl
his jewel   his joy   kill his own she-child
virgin-blood   father-guilt   griming the godstone

Can I choose either   without doing evil
leave the fleet in the lurch   shirker   deserter.
let down the Allies   we've all sworn allegiance

They're asking for blood   it's right what they're asking

a virgin's blood only will calm the wind's bluster

So be it then   daughter!   there's no other way

Necessity   he kneels to it   neck into the yokestrap
the General   harnessed to what he can't change
and once into harness his whole life-lot lurches
towards the unspeakable horror   the crime

so men get gulled   get hauled into evil
recklessness starts it   then there's no stopping

so a Father can take his own she-child take her
and kill her   his she-child   his own flesh and blood

The war-effort wants it   the war-effort gets it
the war for one woman   the whore-war   the whore-war

a virgin's blood launches ships off to Troy

Her shrillings   beseechings   her cries   Papa   Papa
Iphigeneia   a virgin   a virgin

what's a virgin to hawks and to war-lords?

He says a god-plea   her father   her *father*   then orders
attendants to hoist her   up   on to the godstone

she bends herself double   beseeching Papa   Papa
wraps her clothes round her   making it harder
up   up   she gets hoisted   like a goat to the godstone

a gag in her mouth   her lovely mouth   curbed like a horse's
so that his bloodclan's not blasted by curses

her garments stream groundwards   the looseflow of saffron
cloth drifting   cloth trailing   she darts them all glances
that go through their hearts   deep into them   wounding

a painting   a sculpture   that seems to be speaking
seeking to say things   but locked in its stone

they know what her eyes say   that gang round the godstone

often they'd seen her   at meals with her father
in the place beside his   when they sat at his table
the welcoming table of King Agamemnon

she sat beside him   his innocent she-child
singing the lyresong after libations
the melodious gracethanks   to Zeus   the Preserver

What came next   didn't see   so can't tell you

What Calchas foretold all came to fulfilment

Suffering comes first   then after awareness

The future's the future   you'll know when it's here
foreseeing the future's to weep in advance

The present's cnough   and what's going to happen
let it be what we've hoped for   us   the poor remnants
so long the sole bulwark of monarchless Argos

Enter CLYTEMNESTRA.

The Ballad of the Geldshark
FROM *Agamemnon*

CHORUS.
'Geldshark Ares god of War
broker of men's bodies
usurer of living flesh
corpse-trafficker that god is –

give to WAR your men's fleshgold
and what are your returns?
kilos of cold clinker packed
in army-issue urns

wives   mothers   sisters   each one scans
the dogtags on the amphorae

which grey ashes are my man's?
they sift the jumbled names and cry:

my husband sacrificed his life

my brother's a battle-martyr

aye, for someone else's wife –

Helen, whore of Sparta!

whisper   mutter   belly-aching
the people's beef and bile: *this war's
been Agamemnon's our clanchief's making,
the sons of Atreus and their "cause".*

Where's my father   husband   boy?
where do all our loved ones lie?
six feet under near the Troy
they died to occupy.'

FROM *Agamemnon*

Enter HERALD.

HERALD.
 Homesoil! Argos ground! Clanland! Home!
 A ten year absence ends in this bright dawn.
 Most hopes were shipwrecked. One scraped back safe,
 the hope that I'd make it back home here to die,
 die, and find rest in the earth I most cherish.
 Earth   Earth   Sun   Sun!
 Zeus   godchief   highest of he-gods
 Apollo   godseer   Pythian prophet
 those arrowshafts shot at us, hold back the volleys
 god-aggro enough on the banks of Scamander.
 Now be the cure-all, the soul-salve Apollo.
 Hermes, he-god, and herald to godclans,
 guardian of heralds to men down below,
 and heroes under whose gaze we were drafted,
 welcome us back, those few spared the spearthrust.
 House of our clanchiefs, homes of my bloodkin,
 thronestones and godstones facing the sun's glare,
 if ever you once did, welcome your king back,
 look on him with kind eyes after his absence.
 Like a bright firebrand blazing through darkness
 to stop us all stumbling, King Agamemnon.
 Welcome him warmly. He's earned your warm welcome.
 He swung the god-axe, Zeus the Avenger's,
 tore Troy's roots up, dug her earth over,
 her god-shrines shattered, her altars all gutted,
 fruitful earth scorched into futureless dustbowls,
 an empire gone putrid and tossed on time's midden.
 Troy's neck got his yoke on, your clanchief's,
 first he-child of Atreus, most lucky of life-lot,
 worthier than any of the honours he's taken.
 I doubt raper Paris thought it was worth it.
 The town he brought doom on won't boast of his bridesnatch.
 Branded for wife-theft he'd lost what he plundered,
 his ancestral bloodclan razed root and branch.
 Priam's sons paid for it. An eye for an eye,
 or more like ten thousand eyes for each one.

1. CHORUS. Welcome Herald! You're home. The war's far behind. ⌉
   HERALD. I kept alive for this. Now death I don't mind. ⌋

2. CH. Did you long for your home here back at the war? ⌉
   HE. What else do you think my weeping is for? ⌋

3. CH. You could say it was sweet, in a way, your disease. ⌉
   HE. Sweet? A disease! What riddles are these? ⌋

4. CH. That longing you had. We caught it here too. ⌉
   HE. You longed for us as we longed for you? ⌋

5. CH. So much that our gloom made us groan with despair. ⌉
   HE. What made you so gloomy? Our being out there? ⌋

6. CH. It's best for our safety if no more is said. ⌉
   HE. With the clanchiefs away what caused you this dread?
   CH. Like you we too wouldn't mind being dead. ⌋

HERALD.
　　Suffering. Suffering only the gods escape it entirely.
　　If you'd known firsthand our louse-ridden billets,
　　cramped berths on board, claustrophobic, foul bedding,
　　what didn't we have to complain of you tell me.
　　Ashore was no better. Worse. We bivouaced
　　under the walls with the enemy firing.
　　Drenched either by drizzle or dew from the ground.
　　Clothes mouldy with mildew. Locks crawling with lice.

　　First unbearable cold, snow blowing off Ida,
　　blizzards killing birdflocks frozen in flight.
　　Then heat! and even the ocean seemed stifled,
　　slumped, zephyrless, in unruffled siestas,
　　slack billows lolling in the deadest of doldrums.

　　But why go on? What's the point? The pain's over,
　　and for the dead so over and done with,
　　they'll never lust after a life-lot again.
　　The dead are dead. Who wants a head-count?
　　Why should the living scratch open old scabs.
　　We've left it behind us. Goodbye to all that!
　　We're what's left. There's some good for the living.
　　The pain and the losses don't quite overbalance.
　　We can shout out to the universe proudly:

The bloodclans of Argos in battle alliance
having mashed into ashes Asia's town Troy
now nail up these god-spoils to Hellas's he-gods.

For all that we'll get the credit and praises
and Zeus the god's whale's share. He made it happen.

That's all. That's all there is for the telling.

CHORUS.
  Your news shows me that I was mistaken.
  But you're never too old to learn a new lesson.
  Clytemnestra, she should be the first to hear the whole story.
  The leftovers and the scraps of it satisfy me.

Enter CLYTEMNESTRA.

CLYTEMNESTRA.
  I started my triumph cry some time ago
  when the first flame-messenger arrived in the darkness
  proclaiming the capture and downfall of Troy.
  And what did the men say? 'Just like a woman!
  One beacon, that's all, and she thinks Troy's been captured.'
  Mutterings like that made me feel stupid.
  I went on with the sacrifice in spite of their moaning
  then the whole city began 'behaving like women'
  raising the triumph cry 'shouting and bawling'
  feeding the thankfires almost to bursting.
  And why should you tell me anything further?
  I'll have the whole tale from the mouth of my manlord.
  And it's his welcome now that must be fully prepared.
  No day in the life of woman's sweeter than that one
  when she flings the door open to welcome her manlord,
  her manlord brought safely back from the war.
  Go. Tell him come quickly. He's loved by his people.
  Tell him he'll find his wife faithful and bond-true
  as when he first left her, and, like a good bloodhound,
  his loyal servant, and his enemies' foe.
  He'll find all his treasures still with his seal on.
  Tell him I've accepted no man's attentions.
  I'm no more a breaker of bedbond,
  than, as a woman, I wield a man's weapon.

Exit CLYTEMNESTRA.

CHORUS.
>All the words of the woman are clear enough
>if those who are listening give all their ears.
>*(To Herald.)*
>Herald, what about Menelaus our other clanchief?
>You haven't said he's home safe as well.

1. HE. Falsehood is something fair lies never hide.
   The mask of glad messenger just wasn't mine.
   CH. Skins can be fair and the fruit bad inside.
   Can't good news and truth ever share the same vine?

2. HE. Menelaus, he's missing that clan-chief of yours.
   He's gone, his ship's gone. And *this* is all true.
   CH. He set sail with you though when the force left Troy's shore:
   Did a sudden storm blow up and snatch him from view?

3. HE. Storm! Yes, you've hit the bull's eye!
   'Storm' 's a small word that encompasses hell.
   CH. Is he still living, or else did the chief die?
   Is there anyone there in the fleet who can tell?

4. HE. No one knows anything, at least not us men,
   only the sun that looks down from the sky.
   CH. How did the storm start? Why did it? When?
   Was it some godgrudge, and if a grudge, why?

HERALD.
>A godgrudge! A godgrudge! Don't drag in *those* she-gods!
>Some gods preside over pleasures, some pain.
>Those she-gods go with the most galling god-grudge.
>This day's a homecoming meant to be happy.
>When a clan messenger's arrived shedding tears
>to announce to his bloodclan what they've been dreading,
>the rout of their armies, a mountainous death-toll,
>with anguish for all in the rolls of the fallen,
>the best lads in their tonloads tangled and landed
>and gashed by the flesh-hook, the fish-gaff of Ares,
>gaff-flukes and grapnel barbs gory with fleshbits –
>if he comes so overbalanced with trouble
>then that's the time to start hymning the Furies.
>But if the news is good that he's bringing
>and the city's wild with relief and success
>who wants to be first to get the good curdled

and blurt it all out: 'Shipwreck. Shrewgrudge!
The grudges of she-gods shattered the Greek ships.'

Flame and salt water are scarcely a bloodbond.
This time they were though, elements merging,
and their bond-proof – smashing our ships into splinters.
Blackness. Waveforce. Sea heaving and swelling.
Fierce thrashing galesqualls whistling from Thrace,
hurricanes blasting, rain lashing and pelting,
ship-prow smashing ship-prow, horned beast goring beast,
beasts with their horns locked butting each other.
You know when a collie not used to its charges
scatters the daft sheep every direction,
colliding, collapsing, that kind of chaos...
well that's how the waves were. Next morning
the Aegean had mushroomed with corpses and shipwreck.
Our ship though, amazing, still whole and undamaged.
Some god interceded, got our ship a pardon.
Our helm had been guided by the hand of some he-god.
Our ship was one that didn't get shattered.
Couldn't believe it, escaping that wave-grave,
couldn't believe our life-lot so lucky.
We were shocked in the clear light of morning,
chewing the cud of the nightmare we'd lived through.
If any of the others survived they'll be thinking
we're finished, finished, as we still do of them.
May everything still turn out for the better.
Menelaus, let's suppose that he's made it,
let's hope he's still somewhere under the sunlight.
Zeus can't want the whole bloodclan blasted.
That's the truth you wanted. You've got it all now.

CHORUS.
    HELEN wrecker HELEN Hell
    the one who first named her knew what was fated –
    HEL- a god guided his tongue right -EN
    HEL- spear-bride gore-bride war-whore -EN
    HEL- ship-wrecker man-breaker Troy-knacker -EN

LYSISTRATA.
    Since Hiroshima what we've done
    paradoxically's to make the whole earth one.
    We all look down the barrel of the same cocked gun.
    One target, in one united fate
    nuked together in some hyperstate.
    So Greece is Greenham, Greenham Greece,
    Poseidon is Poseidon, not just for this piece.
    Not just all places, all human ages too
    are dependent on the likes of us and you.
    In the Third World War we'll destroy
    not only modern cities but the memory of Troy,
    stories that shaped the spirit of our race
    are held in the balance in this missile base.
    Remember, if you can, that with man goes the mind
    that might have made sense of the History of Mankind.
    It's a simple thing to grasp: when we're all dead
    there'll be no further pages to be read,
    not even leaflets, and no peace plays like these
    no post-holocaust Aristophanes.
    So if occasionally some names are new
    just think of the ground that's under you.
    If we're destroyed then we
    take with us Athens 411 BC.
    The world till now up to the last minute
    and every creature who was ever in it
    go when we go, everything men did or thought
    never to be remembered, absolutely nought.

    No war memorials with names of dead on
    because memory won't survive your Armageddon.
    So Lysistrata – [   ]* – it's one name.
    Since 1945 past and present are the same.
    And it doesn't matter if it's 'real' or a play –
    imagination and reality both go the same way.
    So don't say it's just a bunch of ancient Greeks.
    It's their tears that will be flowing down your cheeks.

* *Name of actress playing Lysistrata inserted here.*

So where we are, Greenham, ancient Greece,
doesn't matter. Their fates depend on Peace.
We've heard you men plan world-wide Apocalypse
and we went on serving dinner with sealed lips.
We went on sitting with our knitting in our laps
while you moved model missiles on your maps.
We heard the men's low murmur over their moussaka
and knew the world's future was growing a lot darker.
Serving the coffee we heard dark hints
of coming holocaust with after-dinner mints.
All this time supportive to the last
we nailed our colours to your macho mast.
I tried to discuss it with my husband, tried
to say he shouldn't vote for national suicide.
O, hello, darling, did you vote Yea or Nay?
'Me, I'll always vote for Cruise to stay.
What's it got to do with women anyway?
Your province is knitting not national defence.'

INSPECTOR.
 O your husband, Mrs Strata, seems a man of sense!

LYSISTRATA.
 A man of sense, all right, if you can call
sense, wanting to destroy us all.
But male misgovernment grew more crass
and in the end we women couldn't let it pass.
Crasser and crasser, week by bloody week.
We could have told you if you'd let us speak.
You've set the world on a collision course
and still go on believing in masculine brute force.
We were driven finally out of sheer desperation
to devise a strategy to save the nation.
Perhaps it was the day we heard recruiters cry
that able-bodied men were in short supply.
And we decided that there was no point waiting
for men to end the war when it was escalating.
If men didn't want to staunch the flow of blood,
there was no choice about it, we women would.

(A big decision for an ancient Greek
not only not allowed to act, not allowed to speak.)

INSPECTOR.

How can I stand here in the uniform of law
and listen to women, *women*, lecture me on War.
Us men sit and listen, us men submit
while *you* tell *us*, Hell, No, Shit!
Men give the advice and women take it.
Men enforce the law when women break it.
I'm a man. I say. You do. I wear the clothes
that give me authority and you wear those.

LYSISTRATA.

Sexual identity, what a frightful bore
when the issue we're debating is the end of War.

FROM Medea: *a sex-war opera*

The CHORUS OF WOMEN *enter and "bury" the* SONS OF MEDEA.

The DOWNSTAGE WOMAN *begins to lecture the* DOWNSTAGE MAN *and the audience.*

DOWNSTAGE WOMAN.
As part of their hostile campaign
against the old Earth Mother's reign
men degrade her
in whatever form she takes
Goddess brandishing her snakes,
Helen, Leda...

Men's hatred had to undermine
Medea's status as divine
and to reduce her
to a half-crazed children-slayer
making a monster of Medea
like the Medusa.

The point of this projected role
is that it's the opposite pole
of Mother Earth,
and what was once the source of life
's degraded to a murderous wife
destroying birth.

By shedding her own children's blood
Medea negates all motherhood –
grist to the mill
of menfolk who attempt to drag
the All-Giving Goddess down to Hag
and source of ill.

That monstrous patriarchal fib
of Eve being made from Adam's rib
is just another
obviously childish sign
that poor men want to undermine
the primordial Mother.

Evil's all a woman's fault
if we believe the male assault
on poor Pandora
but when the horn of plenty poured
with all the good with which Earth's stored
she was the pourer.

Embattled men had to reply
with gods, male gods from the sky
and not the earth.
They longed to find another
more, say 'male' way than the Mother
to give them birth,

a way where men could reproduce
like their patron Father Zeus
who bore Athena
bloodlessly, full-grown instead
of from his belly from his head
all so much cleaner!

They could dispense with Motherhood
and 9 month pregnancies and blood
and breast feeding.
Euripides makes Jason say
if only men could find a way
of wombless breeding,

and omit that childish phase
those far too formative first days
of nipple sucking
and, in fact, dispense with all desires,
find reproduction that requires
no fucking!

As the sex-war's still being fought
which sex does a myth support
you should be asking.
What male propaganda lurks
behind most operatic works
that music's masking?

FROM **Square Rounds**

CLARA HABER.
    I gave up chemistry to serve you as a wife
    now you betray our science to poison life.
    The beneficial chemistry that was our bond before
    broken when I saw science made to serve the war.
    You, a scientist, a chemist and yet you comply
    with the Kaiser's orders so that millions will die.
    You, who saved Mankind from Crookes' predicted doom
    may send as many as you saved into an early tomb.
    Now the Kaiser commands a chemist to devise
    a form of killing from those brilliant dyes
    that gave my dress its sheen and elegance
    that caught your eye when you asked me to dance.

FRITZ HABER.
    But explosives are chemical weapons too.
    Mine seems terrible only because it's new!
    My gas will break the deadlock, make the war much shorter
    and therefore save millions from the slaughter.
    The explosives with which the war is being fought
    are simply gas weapons of a different sort.
    How many times in school did you hear your class recite
    when carbon, sulphur and saltpetre mixed ignite
    the volume of gas, Clara, GAS increases
    800 times its bulk and blows to pieces
    the canister confining it, and those bits fly
    and pierce men's hearts and brains and make them die.
    So what has brought the war to its present pass
    is simply another way than mine of using gas.
    Sentimentalists assume it's all very well
    if Maxim uses gases as the power to propel
    a bullet through the air, hit its mark, and shatter
    a man's ribcage, but quite a different matter
    if I use a gaseous resource but I dispense
    with the metal missile. What's the difference?
    Don't they both result in death? That's the intention
    of both Sir Hiram Maxim's and my own invention.
    If Maxim hadn't used gas from each round fired to feed
    the next round into the chamber, now there'd be no need

to use my chemical genius in order to surpass
his use of gaseous energy with my simpler use of gas.
Without the gas the Maxim gun could not exist
and no need for me to counter his mechanics with my mist.
The force of explosive gas that travels very very fast
blows heads and limbs off in its fearsome blast.
It's a chemical weapon, chemicals and gas
and yet the scruples of the moralist let that pass.
Make delicate distinctions but, alas,
the essential element of both is gas, gas, gas.
One gas blows to pieces, one manages to choke
its unsuspecting victims with a greenish yellow smoke.
If I were a victim's mother. Imagine being her
I know which one of the two fates for my son I'd prefer.
If one were forced to make that gruesome choice
and my son were a victim then gas would get my voice.
An appalling decision but gas would get my vote
because apart from internal damage to lungs and throat
my boy would be intact, whole and I
would have a corpse for burial I could identify.
It would still be my boy, *mein liebling,* him
not half a helmet and one mangled limb.
It's bad enough to die but once you've died
isn't it better if your corpse can be identified?
Rather than the bits and pieces jumbled up with others
sent home to the wrong grief-stricken mothers?
The burial parties won't take time to pick and choose,
what each piece of raw meat once was or even whose.
Better in your box intact whatever your belief
if only that your mother has the right bits for her grief.
RETURNED IN PIECES is the RIP
of those who met their fates through TNT.
The metal weapon solider than chlorine's
the one that blows man into smithereens.
The solid weapons shatter men to little shreds
they separate their bodies and their heads.
All those solid metals propelled by force
are infinitely more merciful, of course! Of course!
Unlike explosive nitrates my invention won't delay
the end of hostilities day after bloody day.
The war that's now in stalemate will be at once curtailed
as soon as my invention is released and first inhaled.

102

In the future, if you don't, the world will come to see
that I saved millions and will one day honour me.

CLARA HABER.
Honours aren't readily bestowed on Jews.
You're well aware of the Kaiser's anti-Jewish views.

FRITZ HABER.
That's precisely why, Clara, that I can't refuse!

CLARA HABER.
He would never have used you if he could find
a Gentile genius with your inventive mind.
He's known to call Jews vermin and parasites
and thinks of them as Africans and not as fellow whites!
Don't you realise the Kaiser will restrain
his anti-Semitic prejudice while he can use your brain.
If he could find an Aryan as brilliant as you
do you think he'd even bother with a 'bloody Jew'?
You are supping with the devil and very soon
you'd wish you'd gone to supper with a longer spoon.
He or some saner campaign adviser sees
that they can't win the war without your expertise.
Once they've extracted from you all that they can use
he'll dismiss you and detest you like all the other Jews.
Once the war is won he won't bother to conceal
he feels about the Jews as almost all the Prussians feel,
and if his Imperial Majesty permits
himself such prejudice, what hope have we, Fritz?

FRITZ HABER.
I'll convert that supercilious Prussian sneering
into surprised gratitude with a little engineering
Even the Junkers will finally acknowledge
the superior power of scientific knowledge.
And they sneer at civilians and despise us too
especially if like me the civilian's a Jew.
He needs my expertise, and so he reins
in his prejudice so he can pick my brains.
And the Kaiser sends the Junkers to form an anxious queue
to give chemical commissions to the genius Jew
who made the invisible air serve the cause of world nutrition
and so seems less a chemist and more of a magician.

And who will stop the war unless I go
to serve the Prussians as their Prospero?

(FRITZ HABER *releases the first chemical weapons, chlorine gas, at Ypres.*)

FRITZ HABER.
    With my elegant invention I put to sleep
    the unsuspecting enemy entrenched at Ypres.
    As my silky releases hissed and swirled
    for the first time ever in the history of the world
    I have to confess that I felt rather proud
    of the simple device of my suffocating cloud.
    the Prospero of poisons, the Faustus of the front
    bringing mental magic to modern armament.
    Lacework lassoos on the springtime April breeze
    wafted through the Maxim-shattered trees
    that this spring won't see bud or put out leaves
    and curled round the trunk like handkerchiefs.
    And then the doldrums of trench warfare broke
    when I cast over it my magic chlorine cloak.
    I was elated, no, I was ecstatic
    when suddenly the war stopped being static.
    The stalemate that had seemed so everlasting
    I broke through instantaneously by casting
    my green cloud, my magic silken pall
    over the panicking troops and killed them all.
    So non-violent the way the green veil floats
    through the atmosphere straight into men's throats.
    All that Maxim weaponry so brash, so crude, so loud
    was brought to a standstill by a quiet hissing cloud.
    A hiss like a nest of knotted snakes,
    a waft of silken veils, the frontline breaks.
    My escaping cloud like a scarf out of a hat
    a chorus line of canisters, and that *could* have been that.
    The British line was broken we could have forced a way
    straight through the enemy and as far as Calais.
    Yesterday we could have had the British beat
    never had a gap been so complete.
    But the military *Dummkopfs* threw away
    the opportunity that I gave them only yesterday.
    They lost the advantage and things soon went back
    to the way they were before the gas attack.

I thought as I watched my cloud of doom descend
that my genius would bring the war to a quick end
and by hastening the outcome I would save
half of Europe from an early grave.
I made the opening. They threw away
a chance that might have got them to Calais.
I made the opening. But to complete the task
the German army needed a good protective mask.
The expert in this field, the one who knew
being a physiologist, exactly what to do
was, as it happens, like myself a Jew
and the military prejudice wouldn't let them use,
more than absolutely necessary, any Jews.
I was 'absolutely necessary' but the task
was aborted without my colleague's mask.
So because of prejudice in High Command
the army didn't gain the upper hand
but having depended on the genius of one Jew
they didn't want to feel obliged to two.
By the time the gas had cleared the chance was missed.
The enemy recovered and was ready to resist.
Now to retain the needed factor of surprise
ingenuity is forced now to devise
novel venoms to let into the skies.

(He pauses to register the enormity of the prospect of gas escalation. Now he has to return and face CLARA.)

I am the father of the new era that's begun
since I've shown the world a way beyond the Maxim gun.

(The VEILED CHORUS *begins to hum as before.)*

Oh Clara, Clara, *liebchen*, what has your husband done?
What have I fathered on the human race?
Now even more deeply dyed in my disgrace
it is my dear one I most dread to face.

(We hear a shot from Clara's revolver. We hear the voice of the dead CLARA *singing from behind the flag.)*

FROM The Trackers of Oxyrhynchus

SILENUS.
> But a satyr, good people, doesn't just exist
> solely for fucking or for getting pissed.
> We're not just the clowns sent in to clear the ring
> we're here to show surprise at everything.
> We satyrs are on hand to reassess
> from basic principles all you possess,
> to show reactions apparently naive
> to what you take for granted or believe.
> To ask the simple wherefore, why, and what,
> to show, for the first time ever, fire's hot.
> We're sort of guinea-pigs for gadgets, fire,
> the sculptural likeness, this new-fangled lyre.
> Of all the gadgets we were required to test
> this gadget made from grape juice suits me best.

> We've all served our time with that weight on our heads
> But no satyr ever trod where tragedy treads
> Gods, kings, and heroes have all walked there.
> High and low divided just by a stair.
> Now's my big chance! Do I dare, do I dare!

(Spotlight on papyrus.)

> ... ως απολλυμαι κακως ...O woe, O woe.

(Enter SILENUS *through papyrus.)*

> Not bad for a satyr for his first go!

> Satyrs in theatre are on hand to reassess
> doom and destiny and dire distress.
> Six hours of tragedy and half an hour of fun.
> But they were an entity conceived as one.
> But when the teachers and critics made their selections
> they elbowed the satyrs with embarrassing erections.
> Those teachers of tragedy sought to exclude
> the rampant half-animals as offensive and rude.
> *But* whose eyes beheld the Promethean blaze?

(In answer comes the shouted response of the CHORUS OF SATYRS *supported also by the 'ghosts' of the 8000 spectators at the ancient Pythian Games.)*

CHORUS.
Ours!

SILENUS.
(Shouting back.)
And whose horse-lugs hear the first lyre when it plays?

CHORUS.
Ours!

SILENUS.
And who kissed the flames and found they were hot?

CHORUS.
US!

SILENUS.
And who saw their ugly mugs first fashioned in pot?

CHORUS.
US!

SILENUS.
And when the first vintage was picked from the vine,
Who watched it ferment, who supped the first wine?

CHORUS.
US!

SILENUS.
Who pioneered the art of getting pissed?

CHORUS.
US!

SILENUS.
Who's indispensable to the papyrologist?

CHORUS.
US!

SILENUS.
Who scrabbled in sand to find bits of Greek?

CHORUS.
US!

SILENUS.
Who pulled from oblivion the words that we speak?
US! US! US!

CHORUS.
US! US! US!

(SILENUS *allows the echoes of the* CHORUS *and the 8000 ghosts of
the Pythian Games to die away, then continues.*)

SILENUS.
We have to keep a proper distance though.
We're meant as Calibans to serve a Prospero.
Deferential, rustic, suitably in awe
of new inventions is what your satyr's for.
But we mustn't, as you heard, actually aspire
to actually *play* your actual lyre.
Wondering, applauding, that's our participation
but satyrs have to stick to their satyr station.
Apollo mentioned Marsyas who lost his skin
and all he really wanted was to join in.
Did Marsyas deserve his awful flaying
for a bit of innocent *aulos* playing?
Your satyr's fine in music just as long
he doesn't think that *he* can sing the song.
To be an applauding punter but not to trespass
on cultural preserves like brother Marsyas.
The *aulos* was Athene's flute. She flung it away
so why shouldn't my brother pick it up and play?
After only a few blows that goddess gave the flute
she'd just invented the elegant boot.
She flung the thing aside. Do you know why?
Think of the *aulos*. Ever had a try?
You puff your cheeks out, like this, when you play
and *she* didn't like her face to look that way.
She thought it unattractive. Well, it's true
her cheeks looked like balloons when the goddess blew.

108

And who should see the flung flute in the grass
but our brother satyr, Marsyas?
Questions of cosmetics scarcely matter
to one who has the ugly mug of a satyr.
It wasn't for good looks that Marsyas was noted
so he blew and blew and let his cheeks get bloated.
He took himself off to a quiet bit of wood
and girned and puffed and grunted and got *good*.
Can't you hear the Muses on Parnassós say
'Who gave a common satyr licence to play?'
Music's an inner circle that has to exclude
from active participation a beast so crude.

'How can *he* be a virtuoso on the flute?
Look at the hoofs on him. He's half a brute!'
His one and only flaw. He showed that flutes
sound just as beautiful when breathed into by 'brutes'.
It confounded the categories of high and low
when Caliban could outplay Prospero.
So the goddess Athene's discarded whistle
turned brother Marsyas to gore and gristle.
And while Marsyas suffered his slow flaying
Apollo looked on with his 'doo-dah' playing.
The last thing he saw was his own skin
like a garment at his feet with no one in.
Wherever the losers and the tortured scream
the lyres will be playing the Marsyas theme.
You'll hear the lyres playing behind locked doors
where men flay their fellows for an abstract cause.
The kithara cadenza, the Muses mezzo trill
cover the skinning and the screaming still.
Wherever in the world there's prison and pain
the powerful are paying the Marsyas refrain.
In every dark dungeon where blood has flowed
the lyre accompanies the Marsyas ode.
Wherever the racked and the anguished cry
there's always a lyre-player standing by.
Some virtuoso of Apollo's *Ur-* violin
plays for the skinners as they skin.
And *why* shouldn't Marsyas or me aspire
to be virtuosos of the flute or... lyre?

If Marsyas had touched it and said 'ooo'
the way that us satyrs are supposed to do,
but he went and picked it up and blew the flute
and that was trespassing for the man/brute.
For *them* it would have been quite enough
to have given it just one abortive puff,
a buffoonish ballooning of the brutish cheeks
producing a few, and inexpert, squeaks,
that would have amused them and been OK
but Marsyas, man/animal, he learned to *play*.
To have watched him smell it, test it with his teeth
or use it like the pygmies as a penis sheath,
all allowable, all tolerated fun,
but the Apollonian goes for his gun,
when it suddenly dawns on him the swine
the pearl is cast before by one divine
knows it's a pearl, and not some novel food
and aspires beyond dumb swinetude.
When he enters the Culture it represents
they reach for their skin-removing instruments.

FROM Poetry or Bust

Covent Garden Opera House, London.

Enter A CONSTABLE *who comes to stop* JOHN NICHOLSON, *who is very drunk, from selling his books of poems at the Opera House and abusing those who won't buy them.*

JOHN NICHOLSON.
    But I'm the Airedale Bard!

CONSTABLE.
                              God, defend us!

JOHN NICHOLSON.
    I made the Aire immortal with my lyre!

CONSTABLE.
    You're also drunk and dressed in soiled attire.

JOHN NICHOLSON.
    But I'm the Airedale Bard!!!

CONSTABLE.
                        You're permanently *barred.*
    (Indicating Shakespeare's bust.)
    I think it was your pal here who called the guard.

JOHN NICHOLSON *(being marched off).*
    I'm going to be a bust from Chantrey's yard.

CONSTABLE.
    You're going to spend the night in Bow Street jail
    and sleep off the effects of all that ale.

The CONSTABLE *puts him in the cell and slams the door.*
The door re-opens. JOHN NICHOLSON's *head appears.*

JOHN NICHOLSON.
    I'll be in marble when all of you are dust.
    Tonight I may be busted, tomorrow I'm a bust.

The prison door opens and the sobered JOHN NICHOLSON *collects his bust from Chantrey's yard and runs clutching his plaster bust all the way back to Bradford. His wife* MARTHA *waits for him with her own bundle. Two equal bundles wrapped in white cloth. She stays silent.*

JOHN NICHOLSON.
Martha, Martha, the poems I've written
may start in Bradford but they'll conquer Britain.
I went into the Abbey and saw all the great,
the bards in marble with the heads of state.
I heard their spirits whisper, yea, O yea,
you'll be here with us, John Nicholson, one day.

(Noticing that MARTHA *is carrying something.)*

What's that, our Martha, got a gift for me?

MARTHA.
Yes, summat to inspire your poetry.

JOHN NICHOLSON *(hardly listening)*.
I went to Francis Chantrey's famous sculpture yard
and found the genius who'll carve the Airedale bard;
a genius of the chisel (and a Sheffield lad!)
The greatest bust creator Europe's ever had.
I hear his chisels tapping. It's a sound that draws
me onwards to posterity's applause.
I hear his chisel like a roll of drums
saying O FAME, prepare! A new bard comes!

But to be going on with, Martha, see
look what I've brought from London.

MARTHA.
                                        What's that?

JOHN NICHOLSON.
                                                    ME !

I'll soon be famous, Martha, almost there;
they'll know me by the Thames as by the Aire.
You and the bairns are going to be that proud.

(Seeing the bundle in MARTHA's *hands.)*

What's that, love?

MARTHA.
                    Your baby in her shroud!

112

JOHN NICHOLSON *drops the plaster bust of himself and hears it smash. The breaking of the bust vies with* MARTHA*'s news for his full awareness and attention.*

MARTHA.
> While you were pursuing your poetic fame
> I saw her spirit leave its feeble frame.
> You've gained a plaster likeness, lost a wain
> who died while you were drunk at Drury Lane.
> Her tiny corpse will rot a little faster
> than that daft mug you've brought. She isn't plaster
> though she's cold as marble and as white.
> She was warm flesh and blood till t'other night.
> Call your Francis Chantrey, maybe, maybe
> he can knock you up a marble baby.
> I sometimes think that you'd prefer
> a marble likeness to the living her.
> You wouldn't need to work to earn a crust
> to feed a never hungry marble bust.
> Nay, flesh with all its hungers can't compete
> with marble busts. Busts don't have to eat.
> Isn't it sad, my lass, tha didn't last to
> plant a kiss on daddy cast in plaster.
> Well, John Nicholson, your fame has come too late
> for little Martha. Martha couldn't wait.
> Here's your daughter, Martha, dead and gone.

> What can she ever be? A poem by Nicholson?

Long silence from JOHN NICHOLSON.

JOHN NICHOLSON.
> She will. The least a poet can do's
> commit her memory to the caring Muse.

FIVE

A Kumquat for John Keats

Today I found the right fruit for my prime,
not orange, not tangelo, and not lime,
nor moon-like globes of grapefruit that now hang
outside our bedroom, nor tart lemon's tang
(though last year full of bile and self-defeat
I wanted to believe no life was sweet)
not the tangible sunshine of the tangerine,
and no incongruous citrus ever seen
at greengrocers' in Newcastle or Leeds
mis-spelt by the spuds and mud-caked swedes,
a fruit an older poet might substitute
for the grape John Keats thought fit to be Joy's fruit,
when, two years before he died, he tried to write
how Melancholy dwelled inside Delight,
and if he'd known the citrus that I mean
that's not orange, lemon, lime or tangerine,
I'm pretty sure that Keats, though he had heard
'of candied apple, quince and plum and gourd'
instead of 'grape against the palate fine'
would have, if he'd known it, plumped for mine,
this Eastern citrus scarcely cherry size
he'd bite just once and then apostrophise
and pen one stanza how the fruit had all
the qualities of fruit before the Fall,
but in the next few lines be forced to write
how Eve's apple tasted at the second bite,
and if John Keats had only lived to be,
because of extra years, in need like me,
at 42 he'd help me celebrate
that Micanopy kumquat that I ate
whole, straight off the tree, sweet pulp and sour skin –
or was it sweet outside, and sour within?

114

For however many kumquats that I eat
I'm not sure if it's flesh or rind that's sweet,
and being a man of doubt at life's mid-way
I'd offer Keats some kumquats and I'd say:
You'll find that one part's sweet and one part's tart:
say where the sweetness or the sourness start.
I find I can't, as if one couldn't say
exactly where the night became the day,
which makes for me the kumquat taken whole
best fruit, and metaphor, to fit the soul
of one in Florida at 42 with Keats
crunching kumquats, thinking, as he eats
the flesh, the juice, the pith, the pips, the peel,
that this is how a full life ought to feel,
its perishable relish prick the tongue,
when the man who savours life 's no longer young,
the fruits that were his futures far behind.
Then it's the kumquat fruit expresses best
how days have darkness round them like a rind,
life has a skin of death that keeps its zest.

History, a life, the heart, the brain
flow to the taste buds and flow back again.
That decade or more past Keats's span
makes me an older, not a wiser man,
who knows that it's too late for dying young,
but since youth leaves some sweetnesses unsung,
he's granted days and kumquats to express
Man's Being ripened by his Nothingness.
And it isn't just the gap of sixteen years,
a bigger crop of terrors, hopes and fears,
but a century of history on this earth
between John Keats's death and my own birth –
years like an open crater, gory, grim,
with bloody bubbles leering at the rim;
a thing no bigger than an urn explodes
and ravishes all silence, and all odes,
Flora asphyxiated by foul air
unknown to either Keats or Lemprière,
dehydrated Naiads, Dryad amputees
dragging themselves through slagscapes with no trees,
a shirt of Nessus fire that gnaws and eats
children half the age of dying Keats...

Now were you twenty five or six years old
when that fevered brow at last grew cold?
I've got no books to hand to check the dates.
My grudging but glad spirit celebrates
that all I've got to hand 's the kumquats, John,
the fruit I'd love to have your verdict on,
but dead men don't eat kumquats, or drink wine,
they shiver in the arms of Proserpine,
not warm in bed beside their Fanny Brawne,
nor watch her pick ripe grapefruit in the dawn
as I did, waking, when I saw her twist,
with one deft movement of a sunburnt wrist,
the moon, that feebly lit our last night's walk
past alligator swampland, off its stalk.
I thought of moon-juice juleps when I saw,
as if I'd never seen the moon before,
the planet glow among the fruit, and its pale light
make each citrus on the tree its satellite.

Each evening when I reach to draw the blind
starts seem the light zest squeezed through night's black rind;
the night's peeled fruit the sun, juiced of its rays,
first stains, then streaks, then floods the world with days,
days, when the very sunlight made me weep,
days, spent like the nights in deep, drugged sleep,
days in Newcastle by my daughter's bed,
wondering if she, or I, weren't better dead,
days in Leeds, grey days, my first dark suit,
my mother's wreaths stacked next to Christmas fruit,
and days, like this in Micanopy. Days!

As strong sun burns away the dawn's grey haze
I pick a kumquat and the branches spray
cold dew in my face to start the day.
The dawn's molasses make the citrus gleam
still in the orchards of the groves of dream.
The limes, like Galway after weeks of rain,
glow with a greenness that is close to pain,
the dew-cooled surfaces of fruit that spent
all last night flaming in the firmament.
The new day dawns. O days! My spirit greets
the kumquat with the spirit of John Keats.

O kumquat, comfort for not dying young,
both sweet and bitter, bless the poet's tongue!
I burst the whole fruit chilled by morning dew
against my palate. Fine, for 42!

I search for buzzards as the air grows clear
and see them ride fresh thermals overhead.
Their bleak cries were the first sound I could hear
when I stepped at the start of sunrise out of doors,
and a noise like last night's bedsprings on our bed
from Mr Fowler sharpening farmers' saws.

The Call of Nature

Taos, New Mexico, 1980

for the 50th anniversary of the death of D.H. Lawrence (1885-1930)

Juniper, aspen, blue spruce, just thawing snow
on the Sangre de Cristo mountains of New Mexico.

The trick's to get that splendid view with all
those open spaces, without the hot-dog stall,
and those who shoot their photos as they pass
might well end up with billboards saying GAS!

The pueblo people live without TV
but will let you snap their houses, for a fee.
Their men get work as extras and are bussed
to ancestral battlefields to bite the dust.
And bussed, but to snap adobes, rubber necks
get excursion visits to 'the priest of sex'.
They stay put in the bus. They smell the pine
not spritzed from aerosols but genuine,
dense in the thin air of that altitude.
They've heard about his work, and that it's rude.
Back on the valley freeway at the first motel
they forget both noble Navajo and D.H.L.
Their call of nature ends through separate doors
branded in ranch pokerwork: BRAVES! SQUAWS!

Remains

(for Robert Woof and Fleur Adcock)

Though thousands traipse round Wordsworth's Lakeland shrine
imbibing bardic background, they don't see
nailed behind a shutter one lost line
with intimations of mortality
and immortality, but so discrete
it's never trespassed on 'the poet's' aura,
not been scanned, as it is, five strong verse feet.

W. Martin's work needs its restorer,
and so from 1891 I use
the paperhanger's one known extant line
as the culture that I need to start off mine
and honour his one visit by the Muse,
then hide our combined labours underground
so once again it may be truly said
in words from Grasmere written by the dead:

our heads will be happen cold when this is found

W. Martin
paperhanger
4 July 1891

On Not Being Milton

(for Sergio Vieira and Armando Guebuza, FRELIMO*)*

Read and committed to the flames, I call
these sixteen lines that go back to my roots
my *Cahier d'un retour au pays natal,*
my growing black enough to fit my boots.

The stutter of the scold out of the branks
of condescension, class and counter-class
thickens with glottals to a lumpen mass
of Ludding morphemes closing up their ranks.
Each swung cast-iron Enoch of Leeds stress
clangs a forged music on the frames of Art,
the looms of owned language smashed apart!

Three cheers for mute ingloriousness!

Articulation is the tongue-tied's fighting.
In the silence round all poetry we quote
Tidd the Cato Street conspirator who wrote:

Sir, I Ham a very Bad Hand at Righting.

NOTES

The notes that follow are precisely that: notes. They aim to help you get started on your own analysis of Harrison's poetry by filling in biography and opening up allusions. They offer some ways of talking about poetry, but they are fragmentary and partial, not comprehensive, the *beginning*, not the *end*, of commentary.

Poetry is not secret or code utterance, but it is compressed utterance. Our first pleasure (and effort) with poetry is recognition, recognising what's *literally* going on in the poem: the literal story the poem is telling; the literal meanings of the words the poet is using. The further pleasure of poetry comes as we learn to recognise how the poet does what he does, how he achieves his effects (and what those effects are), how the poetry works technically, how the meaning is bound up in the craft of poetry. With a poet like Tony Harrison, we learn to look harder and harder at the poet's craft, for Harrison is, supremely, a craft-y poet, and the meanings his poetry makes are embedded in the craft.

When he was an apprentice poet, Harrison set himself the discipline of learning the craft of poetry by 'the imitation of great masters' (Yeats). Now a master poet, Harrison has mastered poetic form. He can do it all: pentameters and hexameters; iambs and spondees; couplets heroic or elegiac; lyric stanzas or epodic stanzas or strophic stanzas; paeans, choraics, bacchaics. We do not need to know any of this to appreciate Harrison's poetry, but if we do, *when* we do, that recognition will enrich our reading.

Other aspects of his craft we *do* need to recognise as his distinctive poetic 'signature': the way he uses metre and rhythm, rhyme and sound. The way he structures the poetry. His attention to words. Harrison knows how to write a line so it sounds like a funeral oration or a nursery rhyme. He knows how to sequence monosyllables so when the polysyllable comes it feels like a clout round the ear: *'You weren't brought up to write such mucky books'* (**Bringing Up**). Writing about stuttering, he can make the line stutter. Writing about inarticulacy, he can coagulate the line. He can stop it speaking. He knows a couple of dozen ways – at least – to put together the sixteen lines of a sonnet so that its structure, just the way it lies on the page, tells its particular story. Musically, he knows how to make *affective* sense from sound:

> The dawn's molasses make the citrus gleam
> still in the orchards of the groves of dream...
> **A Kumquat for John Keats**

He knows how to use words to make dissonance and harmony. He knows a rhyme for every word in the dictionary, and he knows how to use rhyme – as expertly as he knows how to use puns – to align ideas, to make them clash, to connect, to confound. Harrison's obsession with words is everywhere evident in this poetry. Be curious about the words you find here. Don't miss Harrison's sense of humour. As he has observed, 'The Greeks placed laughter on the same plane with thought and speech as an expression of intellectual freedom.' Finally, you might find E.M. Forster's critical dictum helpful with Harrison: 'Only connect'.

SECTION ONE

Heredity *(page 33)*

The poet Stephen Spender (a leading member, with Auden, Isherwood and Day Lewis, of the 1930s generation of socially committed poets) remarks that this little epigraph explains 'the accident of a poet's having been born into [a] working-class family' by offering 'an ironic theory of psychological compensation.' Spender says that he is tempted to regard Harrison almost as 'a changeling, not out of some other social class but perhaps out of Shakespearean romance, sneaked into a cradle in some house in a back street in Leeds by some royal parent (poetry being royal) anxious to disembarrass herself or himself of an unwanted offspring.' Spender is one of Harrison's champions – 'He scores against all comers' – and his remarks are endearing, but they are also ironically revealing. By assuming that the poet rocked in a working-class cradle must be a changeling Spender nurses the notion that Harrison's poetry strangles in the utterance, that 'Poetry's the speech of kings.' Uncle Joe and Uncle Harry are going to keep returning in these poems: the stutterer and the mute are the influences who preside over Harrison's effort to turn 'mute ingloriousness' into poetry.

Them & [uz] *(pages 33-34)*

This pugnacious, funny, grudge-filled and self-ironising pair of sonnets teases the reader with a series of switchback contradictions whose dividing line (as between warring factions) won't stay put. [uz] in the title is the inclusive pronoun of the oral demotic. It belongs on the street. It's *uz*. Yet, rendered in this phonetic notation, it looks estranged. And, put against something in Greek, it looks out of place. Is this poem really about 'uz'? Who is 'uz' if some of 'uz' speak Greek? The dedication to Richard Hoggart and Leon Cortez keeps this perplexing double-act going: the first professor is an academic. He's the Leeds-born author of *The Uses of Literacy*, and one of his chapters is titled 'Them and Us'. The second is self-styled. He's the stand-up comic who 'translated' Shakespeare into Cockney. The first time round, 'αἰαῖ ' is the wail of the Greek tragic chorus; the second time round it's the traditional signature catchphrase of the music hall comedian: 'ay, ay!' Thus, 'popular' and 'elitist' art forms are elided, and we discover that cultural division is artificial and nonsensical. The oral traditions of the Greek theatre and the English music hall are complimentary, not contradictory.

The sonnets work to dismantle the teacher's presumptuous claim that 'Poetry's the speech of kings.' They work to claim speech for the voices that have been silenced by the ghetto-ising of their native tongues. They give names to identities that were erased when their speech was appropriated, like Harrison's dad in **Marked with D.** or Harrison himself in this sonnet. Demosthenes stands as an exemplar retrieved from "elitist" learning. He's used here as ammunition for the "populist" cause. The greatest of the Greek orators, he was born in Athens in 384 BC. By tradition he stuttered, an impediment he corrected by filling his mouth with pebbles and throwing his voice against the roar of the sea. 'T.W.', the Leeds-born schoolboy who's deprived of his name and diminished to his initials in the first sonnet, likewise has a speech impediment, the 'flat a's' that go with his 'flat cap'. At least, Daniel Jones would have called his Leeds accent an 'impediment'. Jones' *English Pronouncing Dictionary* (1917) set up models for 'received pronunciation' and 'standard English'. These were described as 'the educated pronunciation of the metropolis, of the court, of the pulpit, and of the bar' – notice that there is no space for women's speech in this scheme – and these forms were judged 'socially and intellectually superior' not just because they gave 'literary, cultural, and educational access' but because they were 'aesthetically superior'. So what would Jones have made of Wordsworth's pronouncing 'water' so it rhymed with 'matter'? Or Keats' Cockney accent? (The boy is reciting the opening of Keats' 'Ode to a Nightingale' in 'mi 'art aches'.) The bigger question is about the class appropriation of 'littererchewer' by the voices of 'RP'. 'Who owns poetry?' the sonnets ask. They answer 'UZ!' And is the poet one of 'them' or one of 'uz'? He's [uz] [uz] [uz].

Thomas Campey and the Copernican System *(pages 35-36)*
Campey has been with Harrison from the beginning: it's the first poem in the first book, *The Loiners*. Like some latter-day Odysseus wrecked by misadventure Campey trudges the streets of Leeds collecting scrap paper and cracked china. He was the man, says Harrison, 'who – without partaking of this culture – dragged books to market with his bad back, and enabled me to equip myself with a "gentleman's" library' (*see illustration on page 32*). The books on his handcart are histories of civilisation's terminal decline. Their gilt spines are straight, but they're breaking Campey's spine: he too is in terminal decline. *Tabes dorsalis* is wastage of the spine. Edward Gibbon (1737-1794) in *The Decline and Fall of the Roman Empire*, Theodore Mommsen (1817-1903) in *The History of Rome*, and Oswald Spengler (1880-1936) in *The Decline of the West* record a collapse of social and intellectual civilisation such that its future will produce "philosophy" in the anodyne texts of Patience Strong and "literature" in the form of best-selling novels by the likes of Marie Corelli (1839-1924, a sentimental moralist who styled herself 'Stratford upon Avon's other author'), Ouida (pseudonym of Marie Louise de la Ramee, 1839-1908, writer of hot-house pulp romance) and Hall Caine (1853-1931).

Nicolaus Copernicus (1473-1543), the founder of modern astronomy, published *De Revolutionibus* just before his death: the treatise showed theoretically that the Ptolemaic account of the movement of the planetary spheres was incorrect, that the earth orbited the sun and was not, therefore, the centre of the universe. Campey's application of Copernican theory is mere ignorance: but then, Campey doesn't get to read the books he piles on his cart. His bizarre dream fantasy in the second part of the poem – in which angels sing *'angina pectoris'* instead of *'gloria dei'* – revolves around the white marble statue of Queen Victoria that sits near Leeds Grammar School, perched on its imperialist 'thrones' that literally base the city's wealth in its mills on colonialist trade. The St Anne's slab that will press Campey's warped spine straight is a grave slab. The 'dust to dust' he traverses reads as a pun: see the way Harrison ends the line with 'world of dust' – household dust – then achieves a second meaning – from the burial service – by starting the next line 'to dust' in the poem's final lines.

Harrison comments on the tension between form and content in this poem: 'I'm conscious of satisfying the literate cultured reader of poetry'; 'I work to give the reader of poetry maximum gratification.' And he does it in this poem not just with his Latin references and his allusions to defunct libraries, but with Miltonic words like 'Ormus' and 'Ind', words placed there deliberately to gratify the elevated poetic tastes of those readers who can recognise them as Miltonic. This is a conscious ploy on Harrison's part. But gratification is not his single object, for he intends the reader to be discomfited too: 'While the reader is enjoying the sentiment of the achieved literary poem he should be reminded, at the very same moment, that there is a cost to pay, and it is probably some-one other than the reader who has paid the cost.' In this poem it's Thomas Campey who has paid.

SECTION TWO

Me Tarzan *(page 37)*

This poem puts the scholarship boy in his attic swotting his Latin. His mates, two storeys below on the street, are '*Off laikin*' ' (that is, playing). Such is the spatial separation that represents the beginnings of Harrison's intellectual separation from his class and that suggests the separation of "high" art from "low", "elitist" culture from "popular". The poem sets Tarzan of the Apes swinging from his jungle liana in the movies against Julius Caesar recording his campaigns in Gaul. It puts Geronimo, the Apache chief who led the Chiracahua uprising against white settlers on the plains of America's far west in 1885, against Marcus Tullus Cicero (106-43 BC), the Roman orator and lawyer who made an enemy of Mark Antony after the assassination of Caesar. Cicero's rhetoric formed the core curriculum for the Elizabethan schoolboy and for genera-tions of English schoolboys thereafter (see **Classics Society**).

In Shakespeare, Caesar is a 'pale face' because he's a ghost, but Caesar is also the quintessential exemplar of white patriarchal – 'pale-face' – culture. He contrasts with uncivilised 'red skins' like Geronimo in the movies. When he shoves his head through the skylight, the boy unwittingly reproduces himself as a little Cicero. Cicero, old and feeble, fled Rome in a covered litter, and when he was overtaken by the army of Mark Antony, he calmly put his head out of the curtains and instructed his murderers to strike. In one version of the story, Cicero was decapitated, and now the boy seems to decapitate himself when he puts his head through the skylight. Only his head shows. He presents a bizarre spectacle to his mates, and to us. He is apart – that is, separated – from his gang. But he looks literally 'apart', chopped in two. The poet –

not the boy – seems to offer up this image for further symbolic speculation. The head (the poet's intellect?) is cut off from the body (society? conviviality?). Is this a premonition of the poet's perpetual solitude, his permanent 'apartness'? If so, the image suggests both the rewards *and* the dangers of poetic eloquence. Maybe it's by being *apart* (in both senses) that the poet finds the voice to speak as a dissident. Certainly, the subversive puns Harrison plays with in this poem mark him out as a cultural saboteur.

Most conspicuously in this regard there is the cluster of meanings that grows like salt crystals around the poem's strange last word: 'Cissy-bleeding-ro's'. We see the name 'Cicero' unceremoniously taken apart. As the boy is taken apart. The gap that results is filled up with blood: Cicero is bleeding not just from his fatal encounter with Mark Antony's soldiers but also from his exasperating encounter with the schoolboy who wants to be somewhere else. Bleeding Cicero! Reading Cicero makes the schoolboy a 'cissy', and he resents being 'Cissy-ro'. And yet, the image he presents out the skylight says that the boy *is* Cicero!

By splitting and splicing words and ideas in this way, Harrison sabotages original meanings and renegotiates new ones. He produces at the end of this poem a reticent ambivalence that is almost impossible to decipher: it is entirely bound up in the strangeness, the funniness but the grotesqueness, of that word 'Cissy-bleeding-ro's'. We can't, finally, exhaust the image by analysis. But we need to be aware that this breaking apart of language and freedom of word formation is a tactic Harrison is going to employ habitually. It is part of his overall strategy to make us look at words and how they work. So one of the things we should notice in this poem is that, for all his hours in solitary confinement with Caesar and Cicero, the scholarship boy is still speaking his native tongue: '*ah've gorra Latin prose.*'

The artist Beth Smith illustrated this poem in a painting, part of which is reproduced on the cover of *Permanently Bard*. Her imagination fleshes out the poet's: notice the wreath of bay leaves that circles the boy's head. Bay crowned both the triumphant athlete and the poet. Because its leaf never yellows, it represents undying fame.

Wordlists I & II *(pages 38-39)*

Joseph Wright, quoted in the epigraph delivering his last words, was born in Bradford and worked in a wool mill as a boy but became professor of comparative philology at Oxford and the editor of the *Dialect Dictionary*. Comparative philology is the topic of these sonnets: street language versus educated language; the biblical 'harlot' versus the street corner 'pro' (= prostitute); the way what's picked up '*off laikin*'' always gets in before what's formally taught. So the tabloid newspaper, *The Sunday Pictorial*, with its timid instructions on human reproduction and its anatomically incomplete stick figures carries yesterday's news to the lad who learned it '*out tartin*'' years before. Still, he doesn't know the name of that mysterious 'summat' in the drawer that in **Punchline** will turn out to hide *another* secret, a plectrum.

Strange-sounding words like 'plectrum' are ones the boy will learn from the dictionaries (and the lexicographers who edited them) that he so assiduously piles up in Part II: the *OED* is the *Oxford English Dictionary*. Liddell and Scott edited the Greek lexicon; Lewis and Short, the Latin, Harrap the French and Abraham the dictionary of African languages. 'Slovník' is the Czech word for dictionary. If a working-class household owned a dictionary in the 1940s it was bound to be *Funk & Wagnalls*.

Words are power in these poems: the dictionary is 'A bible paper bomb' that you can 'rifle'. But they are also, as in a later poem, dividers. 'Mi mam' can't tell him what a 'harlot' is. She doesn't know the word. He learns it, along with 'wordlists' culled from all those dictionaries. Only then he discovers he's forgotten 'the tongue that once I used to know...mi mam's'. The final couplet in the second sonnet and the dangling italicised line in the first pack an uncertain emotional punch in these poems. The deliberate linguistic strategy of these poems which are *about* dictionaries is, by the end, to send us *to* the dictionary. 'Duciloquy' and 'glossolalia' are words we have to look up.

Breaking the Chain *(page 39)*
'Chain' puns on 'chain' as in 'chain letter' but also perhaps on 'ball and chain'. Expectation is a chain that parents throw round their children's hearts. The sonnet records the poignant, pathetic aspirations of a class that wants to better their children but not to lose them. Aspiration is costly: a 'chain' of fathers is in hock each to the next for a whole week's wages to buy the draughtsman's instruments – the 'dividers' – that they hope will put their sons in white collars and ties, not overalls. Parental aspiration is not just costly. It's mystifying: the boy is woken up in the dead of night to get this present that's wrapped up in the sporting newspaper that emerges as Mr Harrison's only serious reading. 'Dividers' in the

final line comes to stand as a painful metaphor that measures the gap between the poet and his parents. And yet, by keeping the 'never used, never passed on, dividers' as a permanent memorial to that gap, does the poet in some measure close it?

Isolation *(page 40)*

'Isolation' recalls 'isolation' in this sonnet. When he was seven, Harrison was 'isolated' from his mother. He had to be quarantined for scarlet fever in the isolation hospital in Killingbeck. His mother fetched him home on the train. He sees that hospital again as he again travels home on the same York-Leeds train. He's going to his mother's funeral. Once again he's 'isolated' from her. The tears the long-ago child cried when he had to leave his mother for isolation get choked back in the adult. He swallows his grief in sobs: 'and don't... and don't... and don't'. Finally, it is not the recollection of his mother comforting him as a stricken child with country wisdom that releases the poet's tears. It's the recognition of his father's never-to-be-recovered isolation. He hears his father bleating around the empty house, searching for his clothes which every day of his life, his wife had laid out ready. He doesn't know where to begin to look for his longjohns.

Continuous *(pages 40-41)*

This sonnet starts with James Cagney, the American film star who grew up in New York's lower East Side slums but went on to win an Oscar. His name is synonymous with the American gangster film. His greatest performance was his psychological portrait of the thug in *White Heat* (1949). The poet recalls Cagney in the cinema – where features ran either as 'two houses' or 'continuous'. Cagney was the 'only art' he and his father ever shared. Now, those memories of *White Heat* and frozen choc-ice bizarrely recompose themselves in the materials of the present. The platform occupied in memory by the movie-house organist who played between features on a giant Wurlitzer that dropped out of sight when the film began now features his dad. He's in a coffin, being lowered into the white heat of cremation as "muzak" plays on continuous looped tape. It's a bleak image, that continuous loop, but it is redeemed by another 'continuous loop', the ring that keeps its shape even in the 'white heat' of the furnace. The ring passed down in a continuous line from father to son and father to son shapes continuity in a circle. This poem makes us hear the cliché 'chilled to the bone' on our nerve endings.

Still *(page 41)*

Harrison recalls an exchange that 'used to take place, at least once a year, between me and mi mam':

> 'Get your hair cut. Boys don't have long hair.'
> 'What about Jesus, then, didn't he have long hair?'
> 'Don't talk to me like that.'

This poem is about that argument. It puts two cultures on a collision course in young Harrison's life yet again. Xenophon (the Greek historian, *c.* 435-354 BC) confronts Valentino (the heart-throb Italian-born star of American silent films like *The Sheik* in the 1920s) over the issue of hair oil. The boy in the barber's chair doesn't want his hair greased with brilliantine: it loses him marks when the fingers he rakes fidgeting through his hair then print his Greek exams with oily smears. We feel his humiliation in the alliteration of 'lopped and licked by dollops' as we felt the repulsive unctuousness of 'grimed Greek...with grease.' But his dad insists. We hear his bark becoming a hiss in 'scored...like some slash scar'. The boy imagines one reason for Dad's insistence in the sonnet's second quatrain. He discovers the truth in the final lines. So the 'smears' that open the poem reappear at the end, this time made by 'tears'. The rhyme makes the point. Like the title ('still' = 'photograph', 'motionless', 'yet'), the opening phrase is a pun. The boy is twisting his hair in a childish gesture of concentration. But, learning Greek, he is also showing subservience to an elitist class like some peasant deferentially tugging his forelock to the squire.

An Old Score *(page 42)*

The confrontation between artist-son and working-class dad that squared up over the issue of hair oil in the previous poem is now about hair *length*. We hear the voice of the father's ridicule in the italics. Paganini (1782-1840) was an Italian violin virtuoso, so famous that he was a household name even in art-less houses like Harrison's. He was a sensationally brilliant technician of the violin, so much so that some of his listeners suspected that his art (like the poet's art?) was in league with the devil. Mispronunciation makes a 'ninny' of the long-haired, would-be artist. *'Poet'* italicised in the fifth line is the poet speaking; later, though, the italicised voice is the parental voice. Perhaps *'poet'* picks up by association some of the mocking derision of his father's voice: is 'poet' the sort of 'proper job' you write inside your passport? The poem avoids sentimentality by turning mockery back on the poet: the 'whole string orchestra' that could play background music to his tale of how he's hard done by ironises the tale. But the poem is about something serious too. The 'Old Score' in the title is a musical score but also something to settle. It is Harrison's long-nursed grudge against his father. This pun carries over into the next poem.

A Good Read *(page 42-43)*
Father and son are growing as far apart as the book ends they'll come to represent in a later poem. Here, some of the books (and 'bookies') that come in between them get catalogued. Dad sticks to his football programme and darts score while his son works his way through the whole of European literature and politics (Ibsen's plays, Marx's economic theory, Kafka's short stories). He, too, seems to have a 'programme': 'That summer it was...' And much of his reading (Shakespeare's *King Lear*, Marx's *Das Kapital*, Ibsen's *Brand*) explores the very social divisions he and his father are playing out in real life. In the poem, father and son speak behind their books, but not to each other. And they're using different languages. The son has dropped his Leeds accent. He's picked up a new voice with his new learning.

The central paradox of this poem is contained in lines 11 and 12 (' "the Arts" '). The final quatrain, which repositions art among the people – for a sonnet is brief enough to read on the top of a bus into town – likewise repositions father and son. The father he scorned now returns to the poet as the material of his art. They still don't talk because now dad is dead. But in the poems the poet makes – 'these poems about you' – dad is a book, and he's 'a good read'. It is as writer, not as reader, though, that the poet goes back to his dad time and again: 'once I'm writing I can't put you down.' This pun answers his former jeering antagonism: he can't 'put down' – deride, scorn – his father once he's writing about him either.

Illuminations I, II, III & IV *(pages 43-45)*
In these four sonnets Harrison recalls a time when his family was together – but not together – on a post-war seaside holiday. He uses Blackpool's famous lights, the 'illuminations', as a metaphor for the way he's "seen the light" in his own life. The end-of-pier amusement machines in the first sonnet are mechanical scenes set in motion by a penny dropped in a slot. Harrison's dad gave him a tanner, a sixpence, so he watches the sensational hanging and the ghosts haunting the Gothic mansion over and over until his pennies run out. These 'ghosts in the machine', like some troubled version of the *deus ex machina* that arrives to "fix" the end of

some Greek tragedy, will return as other 'ghosts' to haunt the poet later on. In the second sonnet the electric shock machine gives a buzz that fuses the hand-holding family into 'one continuous US!' You have to pronounce 'us' so it rhymes with 'buzz': the rhyme, like the electricity, connects the family. But the pedantry of the scholarship boy, even as they connect, "fuses" the system. He with his smart-Alec learning shorts the 'circuit'.

The sand-castles the family builds in this second sonnet look like Boche – German – encampments; in **The Icing Hand** those sand-castles have come to look like wedding cakes decorated by the baker-father's 'icing hand'. The pun on 'icing' makes us think of sugar icing but also of the cold hand of death. The fourth sonnet returns the family to its silent kitchen, its silent teas, its silent divisions – 'his football/my art' – back in Beeston.

All of these poems look at dangerous pleasures: the frisson of excitement as the hanged murderer kicks his heels; the tickling shock of an electric current that, intensified, could kill; the painful anticipation as the waves on the rising tide first lick then devour the sand-iced castle; the thrilling, appalling underground booming as the mined earth that Leeds sits on shifts on shafts that might collapse. The poems look at connections and separations: the child who sneaks off from his sun-dozing dad in the first poem has flown off to a New York première in the last. They also look at labour and love, at what lasts and what doesn't: the icing hand that made the cakes guides the poet's hand that makes the poems. The 'shallow moat' of a poem – a literate structure that outlasts structures in sand or sugar – perhaps manages to contain the emotion that returns like Blackpool brine in the poet's eyes before being washed away. These poems are like holiday postcards scribbled with clichés: 'wish you were here!' But they renovate the clichés. They turn out to resonate with profound nostalgia, for they are messages that can't be delivered to the dead.

Durham *(pages 46-48)*

Durham was founded in 999. For the poet, that's a fortuitous co-incidence. 999 is a number that makes the city ancient, venerable. But 999 is also the number that summons the police when Durham's students riot or when its prisoners break out of Durham Gaol. Monks built the beginning of the city as a shrine sanctified with the bones of St Cuthbert. They chose a site safe from Viking raiders who had driven them from their original home on the holy island, Lindisfarne: a rocky outcrop looped by the River Wear. A cathedral – the poem's 'distinguished see' – was begun in 1093; the castle rose at the same time; the university was founded in 1832. These "establishments" of human order stand opposite anarchy: Durham Gaol faces them across the river.

In **Durham**, Harrison uses this social geography as a metaphor. He is interested in the way the city faces its past and its present. Student anarchists (this poem dates from the 1970s), rapists serving life, big-wigs in a town hall motorcade, and butchers hanging out sheep carcasses are neighbours in a city where 'Anarchy' and 'Grow Your Own' occupy the same wall space. It is a city that is presided over by a carillon tower that has been chiming out the passing hours for generations. The clock physicalises time the way the town map physicalises social stand-offs.

The poet's business in the city is seduction. Well, possibly poetry first. Then seduction. It seems the poet has been reading his stuff to some student group or other. (Unlike Harrison's sonnets, which invite autobiographical readings, however, the poet of this poem isn't Harrison; this poem has other fish to fry.) The poet of the poem has a bit of a conscience about the fact that he's using poetry as an aphrodisiac: 'I feel like the hunchback' – Victor Hugo's Quasimodo of Notre Dame. But as in Donne, Milton, Blake, Yeats and Lawrence, the erotic image in **Durham** is invoked to serve a public purpose. It is used to explore the relationship between individual expression ('sex', 'private tenderness') and social oppression ('Fascism', 'the machinery of sudden death'). The poet connects society's disease to love's potential curative power in linked imagery that wonders whether lovers,

> alone two hours, can ever be
> love's anti-bodies in the sick
> sick body politic.

The pun on 'antibodies' makes love ambiguous. Lovers *might* heal social illness. But even when lovers come together physically, they remain 'anti-bodies' that persist in representing social division.

As in all great seduction stories, when the poet gets on the six-five train to Plymouth and pulls out of Durham, he's alone. A 'mnemonic', as cited in the epigraph, is a memory aid, a jingle in verse. Durham itself, compiling so much memory-as-history, is such a mnemonic. **Durham** translates that mnemonic into verse. It makes the city into a poem.

Book Ends I & II *(pages 49-50)*

The first sonnet is fractured into two-line segments; it's as though the poet can't utter more than two lines at a time. Grief chokes him. Father and son have nothing to say. They chew. They swallow. They stare into the fire. Mother is present in the apple pie and the remembered voice. The second poem reanimates the old animosities, the ugly sarcasm: 'You're supposed to be the bright boy'; 'it's not as if we're wanting verse.' They're stumped for words to put on the gravestone. Even now they can't make (book)ends meet.

Blocks *(page 50)*

The self-blame the son felt for his tongue-tied inadequacy in the last sonnet returns, here intensified. As the vicar drones on through his mother's funeral the poet rebukes himself for having nothing to say – in Greek, Latin or in English. But the reading from *Ecclesiastes* ("To every thing there is a season, and a time to every purpose under heaven. A time to be born, and a time to die... A time to weep and a time to laugh...') sends the poet into his own meditation on the turning round of time: '*A time to...* plough back into the soil' the seeds his mother planted in his life. He thinks of W.B. Yeats who described poetry as 'sedentary toil' and 'the imitation of great masters.' Sedentary indeed: poetry for the child Harrison began with him sitting on his mother's lap. Her lap is like the Muses' lap that cradles the poet in myth. And she is the 'great master' he imitates. The nursery blocks his mother used to teach him his ABC return as blocks of stone sitting on her grave but also on the son's grieving heart. He has to move those blocks of stone to say 'Farewell Mother'.

Bringing Up *(page 51)*

The title of Harrison's first book, *The Loiners*, artfully announced both himself and his topic. He's from Leeds and Leeds men are 'Loiners'. But in those poems he's a 'Loiner' who's a 'loiner' in quite a specific sense. They're all about 'sex and history' – Harrison's description. He didn't show *The Loiners* to his mam. A neighbour took a copy round. Now, thinking about her cremation as an opportunity for the book burning that didn't happen then – because 'It was a library copy otherwise...' – he guesses that reconciliation, post-mortem, may still not be possible. Even burnt, the ash of his smutty poetry will stand out like 'soots on washing' against her 'bone-ash white'. Unless of course this final fire lets her see the poems 'in a better light'. The 'well wrought urn' alludes to Keats' 'Ode on a Grecian Urn', and the elision in the next line allows a double reading. The primary sense is 'you, [and] the poems of your child'. But a residual sense is that 'what's left of you [is] the poems of your child.' Still, mam gets the last, stinging word in the poem in a line that stands off from the stanza, as stiff as her dead hand: *'You weren't brought up to write such mucky books.'*

Long Distance I & II *(pages 51-52)*

Harrison's mother died in 1976. Two years later his father's grief in these poems is still raw. He communicates with his son down the telephone. Their relationship is, as ever, long distance. We hear the gaps in the conversation in the empty spaces between the father's lines. The first sonnet manages to convey how irritating the irritations of old age are, and how dismal, how graceless. Why do geriatrics always have to tell us how their kidneys are functioning? Why does the old man have to return the sweets in such a way that he makes his thrift look mean, like a rebuff? At the same time, the son's gracelessness is dismally evident. Lifesavers are an American version of Polo mints. It's a pretty paltry present by any standard, and only thought of at the last minute by the jet-setting son running to catch his flight in New York's Kennedy airport. These Lifesavers – what a joke! They hardly live up to their name.

The second sonnet is infinitely more painful. The quatrain structure – four stanzas of four lines – makes the narrative dispassionate. Each bit of the story gets equal weight. There are no interjections. No alternative voices. What is told is told factually. We don't hear the old man's grating voice, we just watch his fumbling gestures going through the rituals that keep some unbelievable hope alive that Florrie had 'just popped out to get the tea'. The imagery of slippers, transport pass, key in the lock, shopping, is all domestic. It's about the daily round of chores that fill up life. But it's also about motion, and that's set against the *dead* end, the *dead* phone line. The existentialist son *knows* 'life ends with death'. And yet, and yet...

The poem's last lines register the fumbling gestures of the heart that defies the rational counsels of the head, gestures, ironically that make him his father's son. The 'disconnected number' he still calls stands as a metaphor for the emotion that drives these family sonnets. "Numbers" was an Elizabethan expression for "poetry". Harrison cannot connect with his poetry, yet he keeps on trying:

it's the reason for the writing. In the past. Now. And evidently in the future too: he has put his parents' number in his new phone book. They still feature – count – in his life. They will remain his preoccupation even though they are literally beyond communication.

Timer *(page 53)*

The absence of sentiment in this poem is breath-stopping. The wife, the mother, dead, goes 'in the incinerator'. The only whisper of emotion is Mr Harrison's terse instruction that her wedding ring, her 'eternity' ring, be burned with her. It is the totem that will ensure their reunion in 'eternity'. But then the ring won't burn. Lying on her son's palm, the ring reverses its symbolism. Once mystic and eternal, it now looks commonplace; the ring looks like the neck of one of those egg timers whose 'eternity' is the three minutes' worth of sand that funnels through it. Only instead of sand, it's his mother's ashes – 'head, arms, breasts, womb, legs' – that sift through this 'Timer'. So much for Dad's eternity?

The poem's black comedy – the crazy domesticity of the imagery – connects with ancient symbolism. The black-hooded figure of Death in medieval iconography carries a scythe and a winged hour-glass to signify the fleetingness of time. The emotion of our reaction to the poem comes, I think, from the uncertain metaphoric balance between its images – ring/timer, ashes/sand – where the tension is between the elevated, the magniloquent ('Gold survives the fire....') and the prosaic ('envelope of coarse, official buff'; 'cardy, apron, pants, bra, dress'). One movement in the sonnet seems to claim significance for life. Another makes life no more significant than sand sifting through an egg timer. The ring imagery of **Timer** links it with **Continuous** and **Illuminations II**.

Turns *(pages 53-54)*

The title means 'turns' in front of a mirror or in front of an audience, like 'comic turns'. But it also means 'funny turns' like you have when you're not well. Then again, this is a poem that turns against the poet, first as he turns upon his class, then as he turns upon himself. The first sestet puts the child, in his father's cap, playing at 'dressing up', masquerading as 'working-class' in the flat cap that stereotypes the working class. 'It suits you,' says his mother. But she prefers him 'to wear suits' that dress him up a class. The second sestet puts the father sprawled dead on the pavement. The same cap is beside him. It is marked with his initials: such a working-class habit that, a habit of thrift since you had to be able to trace your stuff if it was lost or stolen, but a habit that might be read as a sorry gesture at self-authentication, as if inking your stuff – *every bit of it* – with your initials acquired you a name. The last four lines bite with self accusation. The dead man whose up-turned cap makes him look like a busker 'Never begged. For nowt!' (Notice how the poet reclaims his Leeds voice for a moment: he's on his dad's side.) His dad never broke the silence oppressed upon him by his class. Death's reticence *crowns* (that's a pun) his lifetime's reticence. It's his son who has found speech and a different voice. He's using them to serve the literate elite with poems. He's 'opening my trap' – the one he shut in **Them & [uz]** – 'to busk a class' that broke his dad. The betrayal is devastating. Has the poet become one of 'Them'? Why does he call it '*our* cap'?

Next Door I & IV *(pages 54-55)*

The performance the child attends and the book-token Miss Jowett gives him are both signifiers in the first of four 'Next Door' poems (two of which are selected here). These poems record his father's rising bewilderment as the old neighbourhood, dated by its 'VR' – Victoria Regina – post boxes, changes into an alien landscape that he doesn't recognise. Gilbert and Sullivan's operetta *The Mikado* (performed by D'Oyly Carte, the company who then held the monopoly on Gilbert and Sullivan production) is set in a Japan populated by Nanky-poos, Yum-yums and an absurd Lord High Executioner who's 'got a little list'. Rudyard Kipling has become synonymous with jingoism, but his colonialist, imperialist, white and male supremacist values in (for example) his wonderful writings about India – *The Jungle Book, The Just So Stories*, 'Toomai of the Elephants' – are impressive because they document the convictions of a generation whose cultural self-assurance was not even momentarily fissured by self-doubt. Ethel Jowett belongs to Kipling's generation. The 'thin red line' of her era was both the British army (holding back the "savages") and the elegant upsweep of the copperplate calligraphy that her generation and class learned at school. But now the colonialist tide has turned. Who will overrun the old neighbourhood first? The 'Pakkis' running up 'sarongs' next door? (Harrison's dad hasn't got close enough to his new neighbours to tell the difference between a 'sarong' and a 'sari'!) Or the town hall bureaucrats whose red ink condemns such neighbourhoods to "redevelopment"? These poems should be put against **On Not Being Milton**. Harrison spent some time in Africa and the Caribbean, and he says that it was by living there, being brought face to face with a culture in which racism was *visible*, that he learned to see, on returning to England, our invisible racism – invisible because it's not skin colour that marks you out for oppression. It's class. In **On Not Being Milton**, Harrison declares his class solidarity. He aspires to 'growing black enough to fit my boots'.

Marked with D. *(pages 55-56)*

Harrison calls this 'the most bitter of the poems about my father's feeling of being worthless. That feeling came from the fact that every time he opened his mouth he was brought short and faced in a very raw way with a sense of inadequacy.' The title begins childishly. We hear 'pat-a-cake, pat-a-cake' running as a faint remembered tune underneath it. So the matter-of-fact morbidity of the first line is shocking: the baker's *corpse* is the 'chilled dough' that's going to bake in the baker's oven. Almost immediately, however, the poem draws back from the ghoulish to remake the gothic horror scene into a beatified transfiguration. The 'risen' man with eyes ablaze and light streaming from his mouth looks like some primitive or ecstatic religious painting. But that is not the final vision, for the poet's scepticism (like his father's tongue) weighs 'like lead' in this poem and depresses hope. The transfiguration fantasy deflates into fact. If his father's 'tongue burst[s] into flame' it will be 'only literally'. It won't be some Pentecostal miracle. The 'D' stands for 'Dad' but also 'Death' and 'Dunce'. Death has made him a 'marked' man. But he has been a 'marked' man all his life. Elision makes the 'dull oaf' baker a 'dul loaf'.

Punchline *(page 56)*

The opening exclamation is one punchline in this poem. Father and son never spoke so directly when dad was alive. The son is hitting out not just at a father whose lack of political imagination leaves him disenfranchised but at a system that maps only two or three ways out of the Northern working-class ghetto. You can be lucky. You can be laughed at. Or you can be hit. Harrison's dad didn't have the physique for a boxer, so he went the George Formby route, the ukulele-playing-stand-up-comic route. To a dead-end. The pun on 'left you broke' registers the son's bitterness. The revelation of the secrets sitting side by side – the plectrum and what it means; the condom and what it means – in the secret drawer register his angry wonder at secret lives that never materialised. The final punch is delivered in the final lines, by the averted eyes, the closed fist.

Background Material *(page 57)*

This poem explores the same connected-but-not-connected para-
dox as in **Illuminations II**: the two photographs are separate but
in a single frame; both parents appear, but not as a couple. What
joins them is the absent presence of their son who is not in the
photograph yet *is* in the photograph. And that's apt. In some sense
he has always been present but absent in their lives. The poet uses
photography to think about ideas he will develop in his **Art &
Extinction** poems. The photograph preserves what is dead and
gone: not just dad but his favourite pub *and* his whole era, his
'background'. This image of social extinction is put against a more
hopeful image: the green in the photograph of his mother's Welsh
cottage that renews its green every year, a promise of life. A fluke
of photography makes the son appear in each of the photographs.
He's a gleam in his father's eye. He's a black shape shadowing his
mother behind her on the ground. Does this mar the photographs?
Has their son's art 'marred' their lives? His writing desk sits four-
square as a statement at the beginning of the poem and won't be
budged! By such photographic reversals, the poet is made 'back-
ground material' to the parents he uses in his poetry as *his* 'back-
ground material'. So what is the shadow holding up to its eye?
Merely the camera that is taking the picture? Or something else?

Fire-eater *(pages 57-58)*

Harrison's Dad was a busker in **Turns**; now he's a fairground enter-
tainer. The linked imagery of the ignoramus-as-society's-clown
connects with another idea, of the poet-as-performer: Harrison
pursues a personal mission to move poetry off the bookshelves and
out among the people. He wants poetry to work in our culture the
way it did in ancient Greece where poetry was political, of the
polis, of the city. In this poem, his father's 'low art' routine,
which the poet has to 'nerve' himself to follow, changes status half
way through. The tawdry magician of the opening quatrains is
metamorphosed into something mythic in the final apotheosis of
the octet. And there, it's the poet who has turned into the clown!
We watch fascinated and perhaps horrified as the conjuror's mouth
gapes to produce strings not of words but of scarves. Our thrill
changes to terror though when what comes out is, like the Pentecost,
a tongue of fire, a searing eloquence that gives dumb dumbness a
power to turn the normally articulate into clowns. The bolshie
poet who in **Them & [uz]** hawked up and spat great lumps of
glottals now swallows his past and learns, like 'Adam fumbling

with Creation's names', to speak anew. And humbly resolving to keep faith with that past he promises 'there'll be a constant singing from the flames'.

Lines to My Grandfathers I & II *(pages 58-59)*

Fire-eater ends with a resolve to keep faith with the past. These sonnets, too, commit themselves to remembering, and to re-membering. The pun they make and then remake is on 'lines'. First, Harrison remembers his grandfathers: his dad's dad, the publican who could walk a straight line even drunk as a lord; his mam's dad, the fell farmer, and her stepdad, the railway signalman, both of them men who worked on straight lines. The poet follows in their tracks. But not in their tracks. These poems (like the one that follows them) are acts of self-justification. By situating poetry inside these work histories, the poet claims poetry as *work*. He shows himself in the writing to have achieved – by long and deliberate apprenticeship – skills as important to *his* job as tending the vat or cleaning the tracks was to *theirs*. See, for example, the skilful alliteration of 'Ploughed parallel as print' or 'straight stone... steep... slopes' that shows a technician capable of bringing meaning into poetry not just by sense but by sound. See the deft rhymes: comparisons/Harrisons; baser/chaser. See the artful telling of the story: it's *granma* who's slaving while grandpa swaggers into 'the Duke of this' looking very much like 'the Duke of that'. Such technical virtuosity shows us that we're seeing no journeyman at work in these poems, but a master craftsman!

Remembering is not just an act of memorialising the past: it is a way of authenticating the present. The poet legitimates himself by claiming the heritage of his grandfathers. As he says, he props open his present with the materials – the boot mender's punning 'last' – of their past, and the weight of that past exerts pressure on his present. But he goes his own way. He lays down lines just as straight as theirs, but he discovers a different kind of masculinity than theirs. He works not with machines or barrels or dirt but with words. This redefinition of virility looks back to 'Cissy-bleeding-ro' in **Me Tarzan** and to the idea that poetry is girl's work, fit only for the 'lassy lad'.

In remembering the past, the poet is aware of re-membering the past, that is, of remaking it. He remakes his grandfathers' plough furrows and rail tracks into poetry. And the curious proteanism of words is such that in doing so he refashions the actual material of their lives into new symbols. The cobbler's last is now a door prop.

141

The knuckleduster Grandpa Harrison carried everywhere 'just in case' is now sitting on the poet's desk. It's 'now my paperweight'.

Lines to My Grandfathers prepares us for a reading of *V.*, Harrison's meditation upon the desecration of his parents' grave in which he meets the skinhead who aerosolled the tombstone with four-letter words. *V.* is another attempt at self-justification. What does the work of poetry mean to the out of work? Where does it fit in? What language might poetry speak to communicate with those fluent only in tongue-tied obscenity? Harrison himself puts the poet in his place:

> Next millennium you'll have to search quite hard
> to find my slab behind the family dead,
> butcher, publican, and baker, now me, bard
> adding poetry to their beef, beer and bread.
> *V.*

Self Justification *(page 60)*

What is the tone of the opening exclamation? Sweet incredulity? Sarcasm? Self-derision? The need to justify himself as a poet has been gathering emotional momentum since **Heredity** where inquisitive outsiders looked on with mocking bemusement:

> *How you became a poet's a mystery!*
> *Wherever did you get your talent from?*

And not just outsiders, either. One of the inquisitive questioners he's answering is his own mother! It seems he needs to justify himself to his own *ancestors* (his grandfathers in the previous sonnet, for example)!

In **Me Tarzan** the Latin-swotting scholarship boy felt himself a 'Cissy-ro'; in **An Old Score** he was a 'Paganinny'; in **Them & [uz]** his flat a's permanently disqualified him from presuming to 'the speech of kings'; in **Blocks** the family still couldn't see the point of scholarship 'for a job'; in **Bookends II**, for all his reading, he couldn't improve upon the mawkish inscription his father wrote for his mother's gravestone. Even in **An Old Score** where he declared himself '*poet* in my passport' self-defensiveness seemed attached to the claim. So 'Me a poet!' might be mocking or diffident, or both.

All of those responses have to retreat in the face of the evidence though. Greater impediments than his speech "defect" have been overcome. His daughter, whose leg was crushed by a lorry, went on to run. Uncle Joe stammered, so he substituted printers' 'ems' – lead spacers, used when print was still set by hand – for the *m*s he couldn't pronounce and learned to manipulate by hand what he couldn't wrap his mouth around. In their experience, impediment turned out to *spur* impediment! So Printer Joe brought home 'buckshee' writing-pads from the shop that let the young poet put his first stammering poetry down on paper.

What 'impediment', then, is it that stops the poet? His peers. The lads. Their aggro. The way poetry 'made me seem a cissy': that's what 'keeps my would-be mobile tongue still tied'. The final couplet finds resolution in difficulty: that's exactly as Yeats would have expected when he said of the poet that 'difficulty's our plough', although he had in mind 'difficulty' in another sense. In printer's jargon, an 'em' is a unit measuring the number of spaces in a column line. In order to make the column align – 'justify' – down the right hand margin, printers used 'blank ems' to spread the line. For Harrison, 'aggression, struggle, loss' will serve him as those 'ems'. They will 'justify' his 'eloquence', and 'self-justification' will come through the poetry. The sonnet's final line spatially mimes 'self-justification' as, earlier, 'b-buckshee' mimed Uncle Joe's stammer. But notice how, to achieve such justification, the line leaves 'eloquence' standing alone. Privileged... or isolated?

SECTION THREE

Classics Society *(page 61)*
The title first proposes 'Classics Society' as some sort of elite club – more highbrow than the Drama Soc. or Chess Club But a second meaning begs a question: what other *society* might we imagine for Britain than the 'dreadful schism' between "high" and "low", patrician and plebeian, that the quotation from Edmund Burke in the final line gives us?

The poem is dedicated to Harrison's old grammar school and ironically celebrates the school's 400 year history of educating young men to be able to translate a dead language whose acquisition 'translates' them out of their own language and class. Defunct Latin is privileged over living English in the sonnet's epigram. 'Tullies eloquence' excels 'any Englishmans tongue'. Harrison is quoting Robert Recorde's preface to *The Grounde of Artes* (1543), written in the same period the grammar school was founded and coincidentally articulating the same linguistic principles the school stood for. In his preface Recorde tells his royal patron, Edward VI, that he is loath to translate 'This sentence of Cicero [Marcus Tullus Cicero, a.k.a. 'Tully'] into Englishe, partly for that vnto your Maiestie it needeth no translation but especially knowing how far the grace of Tullies eloquence doth excell my barbarous stile.' English lacks what Latin has: eloquence. English is 'barbarous', base, vile. It didn't become the official language of England until the reign of Queen Elizabeth, and even then state business continued to be conducted in either French or Latin.

But, English, you've come a long way in 400 years! Now boys at Leeds Grammar School are required to translate Latin, the *old* master language, into the new master language – the tongue 'our leaders use to cast their spell'. It's the language of *Hansard*. 'Hansards' is a metonym for "official" language spoken in Received Pronunciation. Volumes of *Hansard* are the official reports of the proceedings in Parliament, so called after Luke Hansard (1752-1828), printer to the House of Commons, who first published them.

But just as Recorde shunned English as the 'base' oral demotic, Harrison's schoolboys are taught to shun the language they 'speak at home'. They certainly aren't allowed to translate 'SPQR' (= *Senatus Populusque Romanus* = The Senate and the Roman People, the logo that went everywhere in the empire and marked the world as belonging to 'uz') into anything 'too up-to-date'. Harrison remembers translating a policeman's speech in Plautus colloquially. He gave the speech as 'Move along there'. His teacher crossed it out and put 'Vacate the thoroughfare'. He imagines his masters clobbering him for speaking 'delinquent Latin back in Rome' in a previous incarnation. ('Antoninus' is cod-Latin for Tony!) Was Latin *ever* colloquial? Not as far as his teachers are concerned.

So the scholarship boy with the working-class accent buckles down and buckles under, working harder than anyone to acquire the language of elitism that will allow him to exemplify and perpetuate the 'dreadful schism in the British nation' that the statesman Burke (1729-1797) pointed to in warning against the sort of class warfare that, even as Burke wrote, was sluicing France in the bloodbath of its revolution.

The National Trust *(page 62)*

This sonnet introduces ideas that are going to be redefined and expanded in the **Art & Extinction** poems. Articulacy is power, both in the moment and in the memory because the word, inscribed in history, means survival, not extinction, for the past. So you need speech today because 'the tongueless man gets his land took'. And you need speech tomorrow, which becomes yesterday, because 'the dumb go down in history and disappear'. It is ironic of course that the first of these apophthegms has to be translated because it is spoken in a language, Cornish, that has been all but exterminated. Harrison observes: 'The language of the powerful ruling class always kills off the language of the class beneath it.' His sonnet gives an example of the *droit du seigneur* arrogance of that ruling class: the convict who is used to win the toff's wager comes out of it mad and *dumb*. The bottomless pit at Castleton in Derbyshire and the derelict tin mine in Cornwall: these are like the black holes of history into which the dumb disappear. The role the poet plays is to 'plumb the depths', to make them echo and holler, to write the books that bring to book the 'gentlemen' who (acting with the nation's trust?) silenced a class into extinction.

The Rhubarbarians I & II *(pages 63-64)*
These are seminal poems for Harrison. But not the easiest of reads for his audience. About their place in his development he says, 'I'd always thought that my life couldn't be written about' – that it wasn't the "proper stuff" of poetry. 'I remember the day I began to change. It's in the poem I called **Rhubarbarians**. I used to go walking with my father near East Ardsley where the rhubarb fields were; "tusky", as we called it. He told me that 98% of British rhubarb came from Leeds. And my Dad said, "Oh, I was in a play once, I was. I held a spear in *Julius Caesar* at school." He said they taught him, as they do in the theatre, to make indescribable crowd noises by saying "rhubarb, rhubarb, rhubarb".'

'Rhubarb' emerges as Harrison's code word for Northern 'mob' speech in these poems, and his recollection provides a clue about the poems' methodology. The poems work associatively. His Dad looks at 'rhubarb' in the fields and remembers 'rhubarb' in the school play. 'Rhubarb' then is the sound the Luddite mob makes in Harrison's first sonnet, and 'rhubarb' is the sound the MET audience makes clapping his opera in the second. ('It wasn't poetry, though,' remarks the poet drily.)

These sonnets are difficult, and they mean to be, for their topic is struggle, and language is hard. The images are clotted. The scenes shift kaleidoscopically, and time slippages drop the reader into different centuries without warning. The big idea of these poems has to do with the acquisition of a voice for those who haven't got a proper part to play – in a play, or in history, or in culture. It's a Northern, working-class voice and to outsiders it may sound like 'rhubarb': 'indescribable noise'. It's a voice that's been put through the mill – literally *and* figuratively. It has been maligned and silenced by a master class. They've used an education system that serves their class interests to suppress the 'barbarian' voice. But it's a voice that is finally – in the second sonnet – going to get a platform, a platform located in a world shrine to the human voice. The through-line of association, then, is from North = Northern voice = rhubarb; rhubarb speakers = Luddites = Harrison's dad = Harrison himself.

The first sonnet starts with the Luddite riots of 1812-1816 (which took their name from Ned Ludd, a simpleton farm labourer who in 1782 or thereabouts destroyed two stocking frames belonging to his Leicestershire employer and who thereby became synonymous with reaction against industrial change.) The Luddites were violently anti-progressive. They rioted in protest against the labour-saving machines that were being introduced into the Northern textile mills. The machines, they rightly believed, would put them out of jobs. They went on strike, smashed the machines, and, in the poem, torched the countryside.

'Gaffers' (bosses) like Horsfall retaliated by using 'blackleg' (scab) strike-breakers. They brought in the army to mow down their dissident workforce. What was it the Luddite 'barbarians' shouted to drown out their masters? Rhubarb? The mob's noise is promoted to the status of 'a tribune's speech' in the sonnet's first quatrain, but in the third it is 'silence... hush', and in the final quatrain, 'It wasn't poetry'. The mob isn't bothering with speech any more. They're afoot. And the menace they're up to is registered in the spooky, almost incantatory sounds of the third quatrain:

> What t'mob said to the cannons on the mills,
> shouted to soldier, scab and sentinel
> 's silence, parries and hush on whistling hills,
> shadows in moonlight playing knurr and spell.

The sibilant hiss links 'soldier', 'scab' and 'sentinel' to 'silence' across that floating 's' – a Harrison invention – in line three. We hear the wind playing upon the hills in the sound the words evoke – the 'sh', the 's' – as later we hear the mob's pikes being sharpened in the fatal slide of *'tusky-tusky'*. This is a poem whose sense is often in its sounds.

In the fourth quatrain the poet slips time. He puts us in a double present: his father's present, his own present. The owl is the city emblem of Leeds and of its schools, and *'pro rege et lege'* is both the school's and city's motto: 'for king and law'. Thinking about his father as a schoolboy, drilled to carry a spear and mutter 'rhubarb' in the school production of *Julius Caesar*, and connecting grammar drills to military drills, the poet reflects that the mobs in 1812 needed no rehearsal to make their improvised '*tusky-tusky*' sound authentic. Harrison, himself a scholar at Leeds Grammar School, is thinking about himself too. He is a son of tusky soil. The 'glottals' that 'glug' like 'poured pop' out of his own mouth echo his ancestors, those first 'rhubarbarians'. 'Rhubarb' is Harrison's authentic voice. And he's going to use *his* 'rhubarbarian' voice to make poetry.

The second sonnet, then, very definitely moves into the poet's present. Harrison translated the Czech composer Smetana's *The Bartered Bride* for the New York Metropolitan Opera (the MET) in 1978. Quoting the George Formby music-hall song (which Formby would have accompanied on his ukulele) Harrison sees himself at the MET in the role of the impromptu band conductor who waved Blackpool rock instead of a baton. (This impromptu connects back to the Luddites' impromptu.) His curiously crafted poetry in the opera 'run[s] to rhubarb'. It's so sophisticated that his dad won't understand it: 'Sorry, dad, you won't get that last quatrain'. But as he makes that statement he realises how much he's *like* his dad. He's the schoolboy mobster muttering 'rhubarb'! The sudden exclamation is a recognition: 'The uke in the attic manhole once was yours!'

Now, the opera's music is the poet's 'rhubarb'. He sees it in beautifully evocative imagery. The musical notes seem to grow – as rhubarb does – out of dung:

> Crotchets and quavers, rhubarb silhouettes,
> dark-shy sea-horse heads through waves of dung!

But if this is too precious, too 'poetic' an image for a 'rhubarbarian' to have produced, the poet takes himself down several pegs. On stage at the MET he has reverted to his native tongue ('mi little stick') and as the MET audience mutters 'rhubarb, rhubarb' and claps palms wildly, he sees himself comically waving 'tusky'. (Is he a *real* conductor, like the real conductor in Formby's song? Or is he a fraud, like Formby's impromptu impersonator? That is, is he *really* a poet? Or is his poetry impersonation?)

The poems' compression, their self-conscious craftiness, the way they bristle with technical virtuosity: all of this "achievement" (like 'achieving' the MET) is also, I think, ironic self-criticism. For Harrison would 'like to be the poet my father reads!'

Divisions I & II *(pages 65-66)*

These two sonnets situate the work of poetry among the out-of-work: among the dole-wallahs and brown ale drinkers the poet meets in the public baths in Newcastle and in a dreary pub in Ashington (hometown of footballers Jack and Bobby Charlton). They think that he, like them, is on the dole (because he evidently doesn't go to work). The divisions Harrison is thinking about are social, political, economic; and he uses 'football divisions' as a focus for thinking about all the other divisions. In his father's generation it was the working class that had no tongue and therefore no political clout. Now it's the work*less* class, these out-of-work skinheads. Emasculated by no work in a culture that measures virility in terms of work, these young men substitute empty signs of machodom, swaggering their aggro in tight clothes and shaved scalps, knocking back the notoriously strong Newcastle Brown ale that's supposed to prove they're men but "pisses" them legless, going on drunken sprees, writing their aggro in aerosol on walls and in tattoos on their own skin. And the inscriptions? How revealing! They leap off the page like off the skin, itching for "bovver": 'MOTHER'! 'TRUE LOVE'! 'NEWCASTLE UNITED'! Yet ultimately how conservative! Like Harrison's father's generation before them, these skinheads are desperately unpoliticised. Notice how the red and blue tattoo ink against their white North of England skins turns them into Union Jacks in a country that has disenfranchised them from the political process. Notice too how the typography of their inscriptions makes them look like graffiti. And like mindless clichés.

Football divisions are just another way of marking social divisions and trapping male energy in imaginary rivalries and slogans that displace it onto 'play' and away from political activism. So the chant 'Newcastle United' substitutes for real power as Newcastle Brown provides the fake buzz of bravado. What happens, then, when the team gets relegated? What happens when the 'rash' tattoo that can't be erased from the skin starts to itch? Where does male pride go? How do its frustrations get expressed?

And where is the poet in all this? His working-class roots go as deep as theirs into a working-class past whose 'rotten props' (like the fading daylight's in the second sonnet) are close to collapse. The 'lassy lad' poet is as anxious as they are about his virility. They might be allies if skinheads read poetry! He's one of them – but not one of them. So while they drink he writes. And they watch him. The final italicised line is the poet's jotting in his notebook, a possible line for a possible poem. The poet is thinking about difference: '*one front door orange in a row all blue!*' Ironically, it's a line of Harrison that never becomes a poem!

Y *(pages 67-68)*

This poem takes a wry look at the British obsession with class divisions observed at all levels – even 30,000 feet above the ground. Shuttling between LHR (London Heathrow) and JFK (New York's Kennedy airport) the poet sits in Y-class (economy) drinking warm Chablis out of a can, listening to the 'chinks of pukka glass' wafting back to them from 1st class. He cheers himself up with the ironic reflection that when planes crash it's the Ys who survive. But he cheers himself *down* by further observing that while the British insist on marking their divisions, they draw a veil over them (unlike the democratising Americans). Hence the curtains. Hence, too, the apt quotation of Margaret Thatcher (wildly recontextualised, though it's easier to think of her drawing social curtains than hanging domestic ones). That the Ys survive when planes take a dive might be read as a metaphor that carries a political message, if we take the plane as an updated 'ship of state'. This poem invites us to read 'Y' as 'Why?'

Summoned by Bells *(pages 69-70)*

This poem makes me laugh out loud. But also makes laughter die in my throat. Chiming church bells wrecked his inner ear (the ear the poet hears his rhythms by) and drove the poet 'E.P.' mad: Ezra Pound wished for German bombs in the Great War to fall on Kensington to silence the 'blasted campanolatry' not just of the churches (like St Mary Abbot's) but of what those churches embodied: a religious Establishment that, along with Establishment politics, was legitimating and sponsoring the appalling slaughter of that "great" war. In 'Hugh Selwyn Mauberly', Pound wrote of 'a myriad' who died:

> Young blood and high blood,
> fair cheeks and fine bodies.

And died for what?

> For an old bitch gone in the teeth,
> For a botched civilisation...
> For two gross of broken statues,
> For a few thousand battered books.

'Hugh Selwyn Mauberly' is the poem that glosses Harrison's and informs its darker purposes. Pound's poem gives a vision in which 'Caliban casts out Ariel' and

> ...a tawdry cheapness
> Shall outlast our days.

There is another poem to put against Harrison's too, though. It is John Betjeman's. Harrison borrows the title of Betjeman's verse autobiography, *Summoned by Bells*, to use as his title. Betjeman, too, invited the bombs in: 'Come, friendly bombs, and fall on Slough...' But Betjeman's view is affable; Pound's is bitterly tragic. And Harrison's conscious allusion to *both* poets makes for the ambivalence of tone in his own poem.

These days, though, the bells that plague the poet aren't in church belfries. As the faith of the nation has converted from Christian God to Mammon – materialism – so the old bells convert. ('Cinques', 'caters' are bell-ringers' changes.) Today's poet is maddened by Securicor alarms going off all over the city day and night!

This state of affairs becomes for Harrison the occasion of social observation. The poet has nothing for anyone to steal but books – fifty copies of his *own* book! But the thief can't see *books* as hot property. He belongs to a social class that wouldn't even recognise a priceless Pound *Canto* manuscript as hot property!

Once again the "elitist" and the "populist" grapple in Harrison's poetry (and this time in Harrison's back garden as well!). The serious problem Harrison's poem sets us is to wonder what position 'a few battered books' occupy in our culture. Pound saw those 'battered books' – which included Homer, Virgil, the rest of Western literature: books representing a culture men would die for – as sponsoring cynical "explanatory fictions" that persuaded young men to swallow this heroic lie: *'dulce et decorum est pro patria mori'* ('sweet and proper it is to die for one's country'). Would *we* die to defend the books that are the repositories of our culture's ideals?

Harrison's poem invokes Pound, the elitist poet, but also tells against him. Pound inveighed against a 'botched civilisation' yet helped to 'rebotch' it, for his social preoccupations were far removed from his social practice. So Harrison's poem at the end is an oblique judgement upon Pound. But also upon himself. It is utterly self-revealing and very funny that the poet, upstairs in his study, doesn't hear a thing. His house is being done over but he never

> heard the thief
> being obsessively engrossed
> in rhyming social grief.

This is, I think, another wry way of wondering about the position of books, words, poetry, in culture!

Art & Extinction 1, 4 & 5 *(page 71-73)*

Asked by an interviewer to 'justify' (in the way he uses that word in **Self Justification**) these sonnets, Harrison begins by thinking about 'extinction': the extinction of a species, the extinction of a language. He uses the first as a way to understand the second. It's not just that the language his parents spoke – that *he* spoke as a child – is extinct; it's also that *whole* languages, like Cornish, have been made extinct. As Harrison observes, 'The language of a powerful ruling class always kills off the language of the class beneath it. The poet too is almost an extinct species, and it's almost an extinct idea to think of language as the carrier of our most important messages. It's also about the idea that used to console people, of gambling on posterity – *"exegi monumentum aere perennius"* ("I have made a monument more lasting than brass") – the idea that you can write in a certain style because some day there would be an understanding. Now the future doesn't look that much of a dead cert for gambling on; we are faced with a very real idea of extinction, not only of personal extinction but of the work and of memory, and it certainly takes away the feeling that you are laying up a readership in heaven or the future. That choice, which in a sense sustained poetry for centuries, is no longer open to us.'

The epigraph to the first sonnet makes the connection between works of art and works of nature, and the liability of both books and dodos to extinction. But it also encloses an irony. The epigraph quotes Theodore Roosevelt, who became 26th President of the U.S. in 1901 after William McKinley was assassinated. Teddy Roosevelt had led the 'Roughriders' in the 1898 war against Cuba: he was a bluff, pistol-packin', huntin'n'shootin' man who on safari in Africa bagged *herds* of big game. From him we get the 'teddy bear', after he saved the life of a cub (whose mother he had just shot). Like James Audubon, the American ornithologist and illustrator, Roosevelt exemplified a time when mankind believed that nature poured out her bounty in limitless abundance and that man was the master of it all, bound, indeed, to consume it as industriously as she produced it. Everyone knew that nature's resources were infinite. So Audubon ('Kill em, wire 'em, paint 'em, kill a fresh'un!') thought nothing of using up twenty-five real pelicans to produce the image of one in paint. And yet, Audubon is reckoned a great conservationist: his illustrations, reproduced by the engraver Robert Havell, were printed in several volumes as *The Birds of America* (1827-1838) and went into libraries, reading-rooms and drawing-rooms around the world. Havell's engravings allowed the birds of America to be seen by birdwatchers everywhere. But those engravings also turned birds into books. They made animals art. (A deadening process? The short form of 'engraver', 'graver', puns with 'someone who puts something into its *grave*.')

It's this shift from life into art that teases the poet's contemplation (along with the paradox that to conserve something you make it extinct). As Audubon worked in birds, the poet works in words. And his struggle is 'to preserve once spoken words.' This presents him with a conundrum: 'By using them, do we save words or not?' Is the poet a conservationist or a cannibal, consuming his own children?

In the second sonnet, the poet – killing time between planes in New York – examines a display case full of animals that face extinction (because of those heedless 'killing times' that gave Roosevelt and Audubon their specimens). He catches his reflection on the glass and reflects upon his *own* extinction: isn't "poet" one of those endangered species? Isn't he, like the woolly mammoth, doomed to extinction 'beneath deep permaverse'? Or does language, like Siberia's permanently frozen ground, 'preserve' the dead poet?

The third sonnet, **Dark Times**, doesn't resolve anything. Instead, it asks a question. But the interrogative opens up possibility, and that possibility is hopeful. The peppered moth – *Biston Betularia* – was evidently a confirmed Darwinist: it evolved survival tactics to see it through when the Industrial Revolution turned Leeds black with smoke and soot in the late nineteenth century. The city's fauna died. But not *Biston*. (It sounds like 'Beeston': Harrison's neighbourhood in Leeds.) *Biston* adapted. The white moth turned black, into *Biston Carbonaria*. Now, a century later, Leeds is turning white again. Moss is reappearing on trees and on the cold millstacks that no longer smoke; fish are returning to once stagnant streams. So, asks the poet, if man can turn the black tide back, can *Biston*? Can it de-volve its smokescreen 'Carbonaria' to 'flutter white again above new Leeds'?

It is one of those coincidences of history that so engage Tony Harrison that Karl Marx (1818-83, theorist of political economy and socialism whose ideas about work and workers were so bound up with the progress of the Industrial Revolution) should have proposed dedicating *Das Kapital* (*Money*) to Charles Darwin (1809-82, theorist not of social or economic but of natural evolution) at the very time when Darwin's theory of natural selection was being played out by the adaptable *Biston* in a city – Leeds – that was itself being transformed by working practices that turned its buildings black and its people into stunted mutants.

The Lords of Life *(pages 74-78)*

This poem makes 'Art' and 'Extinction' nextdoor neighbours. The gun-happy, beer-drinking, homophobic redneck whose personal mission in his Florida backwoods behind his shotgun is to put alligators back on the 'Endangered Species' list, can't understand the greenhorn poet who moves in next door. Who reads books. Who *likes* snakes, likes their 'shunting...flesh', their 'sashay' on 'shuffled vertebrae'. The neighbour fancies himself Davy Crockett or Daniel Boone – rough-hewn heroes of the American frontier. But really his self-image comes out of Disney's Fantasyland, and his sense of history would fit – with room to spare! – inside one of those aluminium rings he yanks off each of the Budweiser beers he dumps down his throat. Spanish moss, Chinese kitestrings, Pharaoh's sarcophagi, egrets on 'gator backs looking like hieroglyphics': these images reach way beyond his narrow world of stars-and-stripes-motherhood-and-apple-pie patriotism and his (drunken) American dream.

The neighbour looks at the same landscape as the poet and sees none of what the poet sees; none of the past alive (not extinct!) in the present. Nor does he see any contradiction between his flag-waving, his pride in 'life in America', and his obsession with killing so much of it off. The neighbour, his wife, and the poet in turn describe a space launch from Cape Canaveral (it's ironic that man-kind's most sophisticated science is sited in this primordial Florida swampland). The wife sees the spaceship as a pen, the neighbour as a bullet, the poet, as a snake. But only the poet imagines the scene from God's (or "the gods") point of view: America reaches insanely for the stars while it turns its earth into an abattoir.

Harrison's title ironises American arrogance, that inculcated sense of superiority that makes them see themselves as 'the lords of life'. But it also quotes another famous poem about a snake, D.H. Law-rence's 'Snake'. That poem, too, interrogates masculinity. What makes a man? Beer drinking? Gator shooting? Can crushing? Cock-pecking (the re-gendered version of hen-pecking)? Snake killing? Lawrence looks at the snake:

> And voices in me said, If you were a man
> You would take a stick and break him now and finish him off.

He throws a log at the snake's departing back; what 'was left behind convulsed in undignified haste'. At once he 'despised myself and the voices of my accursed human education':

> And I wished he would come back, my snake.
> For he seemed to me again like a king...

And so, I missed my chance with one of the lords
Of life.
And I have something to expiate;
A pettiness.

The last line of Harrison's poem is equally disparaging of man-
kind's greatness. The 'giant gator hunter' kills 'BUD' – the beer.
But then what? Is 'BUD' short for 'buddy'? Is Cain once again set
to kill his brother Abel?

SECTION FOUR

Sonnets for August 1945: *The Morning After I & II (pages 79-80)*
These poems are constructed from the childhood memories Har-
rison recalls on page 25 of this book's Introduction. 'VJ', victory
over Japan in World War II, was finally achieved when the allies
dropped atomic bombs on Hiroshima and Nagasaki in August
1945. In Leeds, Harrison's whole neighbourhood celebrated. They
burnt the Japanese flag – blazoned with a blood-red Rising Sun on
its centre – on a bonfire that turned it black. Thus, in black irony,
they parodied what happened when the atomic blast, with its apo-
calyptic 'jabbering tongues of fire', blackened the sun over Japan.

In Leeds on 'the morning after' people woke up from the
intoxicated celebration of the night before to a lifetime of sobriety
as it dawned on them what the atom bomb meant. On the pave-
ment the burnt-out bonfire had left a 'circle of scorched cobbles
scarred with tar': and the poet remembering it sees it as an image
that looks back to that bomb-blackened sky above Hiroshima, but
more terrifyingly, *forward* to a future apocalypse that will annihilate
the world. The black circle on the ground is a void, like a cosmic
black hole. The very stars are annihilated. The constellations (Sagi-
ttarius, the Archer; Libra, the Scales) originally named by the
Greeks are gone. Those names remind us that our world is one in
which the Greeks still survive: Aeschylus, Sophocles, Demosthenes,
Xenophon are alive in their writings that we still read. Their cul-
ture survives in ours by the words, the names, the concepts they
gave us: democracy, politics, tyranny, anarchy, sympathy, antagon-
ism. We bear the imprint of civilisations three thousand years back.
So if we destroy our world, it is not just our present we destroy.
We destroy all history – we destroy *them* – all memory, all past.

A reincarnation of that past finds its way into the second son-
net by unconscious, oblique imitation: the child plays Dracula by
the bonfire in the now redundant blackout curtains. He's *'laikin''*.

But he's also performing the rites of the collective consciousness: he's an actor, playing on the verge of what, in the morning, will look like an *orchestra* – the circular dancing floor of the Greek theatre. So his 'play' offers an accidental metaphor that's hugely optimistic, for if one potential future for mankind is prefigured in a black circle scarred with tar that signifies the apocalypse, then another future is potential in the symbolism of another version of the circle, one that's sunlit. It's the circle of the theatre the Greeks invented, a theatre of struggle, of *agon*, where we struggle to learn what we must know to avoid annihilation. So the child's 'play' figures the 'play' in the theatre. That play permits us to play out futures 'in play' that we don't have to suffer 'for real'. These sonnets are connected to Harrison's theatre poetry: they share topics (war) and symbols (the circle). Harrison saw in the 'morning after' cobblestone scorch-marks 'one circle of the celebrant and the sufferer'. In the theatre extracts that follow in this collection, he begins to people the circle with celebrants and sufferers.

Initial Illumination *(pages 81-82)*

This poem was first published in *The Guardian* on 5 March 1991, a few days after the U.S. President, George Bush, ordered the offensive against Iraq after the invasion of Kuwait (and the Kuwaiti oilfields). It shows Harrison using poetry as an immediate, urgent form of public address. It reworks the imagery of his earlier **Sonnets for August 1945**: like the bomb over Hiroshima, the bombs over Baghdad that illuminate the midnight with false light (and betray a cock into thinking it's morning and crowing his heart out) also darkens the noonday by blocking out the sun, by blackening bodies, by blacking out life. This poem echoes – urgent, intensified – thoughts the poet has had before:

> let them remember, all those who celebrate,
> that their good news in someone else's bad.

And it echoes doubts the poet has had before:

> Doubtful, in these dark days, what poems can do...

The poem's central metaphor is 'illumination': the explosive light of bombs dropping, the saving light that may 'never dawn on poor mankind', the gold leaf and vibrant colours that light up – illuminate – the medieval manuscript. On a train heading for a poetry reading on the day the offensive is launched Harrison sees cormorants flying around Lindisfarne, and that triggers a memory: of a seventh-century manuscript of the New Testament, the Lindisfarne

Gospel that is now lodged in the British Museum. In it, the Saxon scribe made long-necked cormorants part of his illumination of the initial 'I' of *In principio* – 'In the beginning...' – the opening of the Gospel of St John. Harrison's thinking about this 'beginning' is ironic as he contemplates the possible end of the world.

What follows from this memory is a string of associations impacted one upon the other: the monastic treasures of Lindisfarne were looted by Viking raiders not so different from their modern counterparts; the 'good book', the Bible, may be doubtfully "good" if it's been responsible for 'in the beginning' religious war (like the one in the Gulf?) for two thousand years; the 'Word' that follows *In principio* in St John has been conscripted by George Bush, as the illuminator's 'I' has been conscripted by the munitions manufacturers who supply the U.S. Pentagon. The 'I' is now the 'eye' marked with a (Christian?) cross on high-tech gun-sights.

The rhetorical interrogation the poet puts in the final seven lines of the poem has a desperate urgency borne on the high pressure of the syntax. He wants to know what victory means. 'Is it open-armed at all that victory V?' (Here's another 'initial' that's being 'illuminated'.) Or is the V sign merely 'crowing' by those 'who don't yet smell the dunghill at their claws'? This poem throbs with pain: it sets man's atrocities against his excellences ('steady hand, gold leaf, a brush') in a world of such beauty (where 'Farne cormorants... shower fishscale confetti on the shining sea'); a world that man has the awful power – invoking the word of God as he does so – to destroy.

FROM *Agamemnon (pages 83-89)*
This extract is taken from near the beginning of *The Agamemnon*, the first play in *The Oresteia* trilogy. Twelve geriatric 'Argos geezers', 'recruiter's refuse' forced to stay behind when the Greek warships sail for Troy, make up the Chorus. They tell the story of the ten-year-long campaign. The 'whore war' as they call it is the 'war for one woman': Helen, wife of Sparta's King Menelaus, seduced by Paris of Troy, King Priam's son. Menelaus incites his brother Agamemnon, King of Argos (they are two of the surviving sons of the infamous House of Atreus) to launch a thousand ships against Troy to win Helen back. Agamemnon's queen is Clytemnestra, Helen's sister, daughter of Tyndareos. They tell the story sometimes factually, sometimes expressionistically and out of sequence. They image the 'wife-snatch' as 'nest-theft   childloss   wild frustration'; the brothers are 'twin prey birds' 'mewing warcries': Paris

156

has violated the guest-right Greeks hold sacred, and Zeus the 'high he-god' sends down a Fury to aid the revenge the preybirds shrill for.

The war's been going on for ten years now. It's in stalemate. But Clytemnestra has ordered sacrifice, as if for triumph. Why, asks the Chorus? Is there news from Troy? (The audience knows the answer; they've seen the Watchmen see the beacon fire that announces Troy's fall in the first part of the scene.) But the Chorus doesn't get an answer yet. They tell more of the story.

From the beginning, the campaign was a disaster. First there was the omen. Twin preybirds emerging out of the blue ripped open the belly of a pregnant hare and spilled the young ones out, with the entrails. Calchas, the seer, interpreted the sign, saw that it meant that a god (Artemis? the huntress? the she-god protector of young things?) was involved, a god who intended to test men's resolve for what they intended to do by demanding that they confirm it with a blood sacrifice. There were other signs too of the gods' intervention. The armada, set for sail, hadn't left port. It was storm-stymied at Aulis by winds whose contrary blasts had to be the work of some god. Agamemnon heard the prophecies. And accepted 'Necessity'. His daughter, Iphigeneia, was sacrificed. The winds changed. The ships sailed.

Telling this story, however, at the crucial moment the Old Men avert their eyes:

> What came next   didn't see   so can't tell you.

But certain truths are known without being seen:

> Suffering comes first   then after awareness

What Agamemnon did is 'unspeakable horror' framed as 'Necessity':

> Necessity   he kneels to it   neck into the yokestrap.

So the cycle of atrocity turns one more turn. Yet the Chorus speaks also for hope out of destruction:

> Batter, batter the doom-drum, but believe there'll be better.

Oswyn Murray, the Greek historian and Fellow of Balliol College, Oxford, calls Harrison's trilogy 'the classic account for our generation of *The Oresteia*.' Harrison invents for it a language that imitates the original: Aeschylus to his contemporaries in Athens in 458 BC was craggy, sonorous, deliberately archaic. Harrison's version writes a language that has the musculature of the Anglo-Saxon English found in *Beowulf*, and it releases the primitive, the savage energies that Harrison came up against in the original. Perhaps his finest invention is a series of compounds that redistributes power equally between the sexes: there is no "feminine ending" in this saga where the woman does the killing, no '*god*dess', no '*daugh*ter', but 'he-child', 'she-child'; 'he-god', 'she-god'; 'bed-bond', 'blood-bond. The trilogy grapples with issues as on a wrestling mat – the metaphor it returns to time and again – and men and women wrestle here as equals.

Harrison describes the text of his *Oresteia* as a 'rhythmic libretto for masks, music, and an all-male company' (see the Introduction, page 12, for his comments on masks). It was spoken on a pulse. Harrison Birtwistle composed the percussive music that set the paces. The shifts of rhythm from speech to speech, from line to line, or from voice to voice need to be felt physically. Individual lines were frequently divided and shared among contrapuntal voices, the Chorus being divided into "teams" of speakers. Such division is notated in the text by the spacing, as in: 'What came next   didn't see   so can't tell you'. The unison speaking of other lines – 'Batter, batter the doom-drum, but believe there'll be better' – was therefore all the more emphatic.

The whole sweep of *The Oresteia* goes from the triumphant return of the king and his revenge killing by Clytemnestra in *Agamemnon* to the return of Orestes, his son, who kills his mother in the second play, *Choephori* (The Libation Bearers). Orestes is pursued by his mother's Furies in the third play, but a murder trial presided over by Athene judges him not guilty. Athene reconciles the Furies, who have vowed to lay waste to Athens in reprisal, by offering them a permanent home under the Areopagus, the Hill of Ares that all Athenians revere. The Furies become the Eumenides, the Kindly Ones, and leave the theatre draped in robes that recall the original blood sacrifice of Iphigeneia, only now grudge has been transformed to blessing. The third play takes its name from them: *Eumenides*.

The Ballad of the Geldshark *(page 90)*

Harrison calls this part of *The Oresteia* 'The Ballad of the Geldshark'. Ares is the god of war who here is seen to traffic in corpses and to trade in 'fleshgold'. The ballad is embedded in *Agamemnon*'s second big choral ode. As the ballad begins, the verse changes, the rhythm changes, and the voice of the Chorus changes. The Old Men ventriloquise women's voices to show what war costs the survivors:

my husband sacrificed his life

my brother's a battle-martyr...

The tattoo beat out in this bleak war ballad fuses transhistoric references that link Troy to Vietnam to the Gulf: the 'plectrum', the 'amphorae' and 'Ares' locate the war in an ancient, mythic past; but 'dog tags', 'clinker', 'belly-aching', 'army issue' put it on the Somme, on Normandy's beaches, in the jungles of South East Asia. Ares emerges both as some Dickensian pawnbroker and a Thatcherite entrepreneur ('geld' = 'money'). But 'geld' has another meaning, so the ballad comes to express a second, absurd paradox. Men use phallic weaponry to assert their masculinity in war; but war spends them, it wastes them, and it *gelds* them in Death. Death is surely the ultimate 'unmanning', the ultimate castration.

FROM *Agamemnon (pages 91-95)*
The first of the survivors of the war in Troy reaches home. The Herald crows Agamemnon's triumph and describes Troy's devastation in post-holocaust imagery:

> her god-shrines shattered, her altars all gutted,
> fruitful earth scorched into futureless dustbowls,
> an empire gone putrid and tossed on time's midden.

But his relief betrays his dis-ease, and the stichomythia (lines traded one for one like volleys across a tennis net marked with large square brackets) between the Chorus and the Herald utters their dis-ease too: all is not well in Argos. As if triggered by these unstated revelations, the Herald's tale turns to recounting the war's suffering, and his bright triumphalism begins to dim. Then Clytemnestra enters announcing the approach of Agamemnon: 'it's his welcome now that must be fully prepared.' She has, she says, been loyal in his absence:

> I'm no more a breaker of bedbond,
> than, as a woman, I wield a man's weapon.

But she's lying. She's already laid out the man-axe, and she intends to use it. On Agamemnon. After she exits, the Chorus presses the Herald for more information. The whole appalling story finally comes out of what happened after Troy fell, of godgrudge and waveforce and shipwreck. The whole fleet was destroyed as it sailed for home. One ship escaped. Possibly two. The Herald's exultation is transformed into despair. He concludes uncomprehendingly: 'Zeus can't want the whole bloodclan blasted.' Can he? He leaves, utterly dejected. The Chorus reacts to the tale with what looks like *non sequitur*:

HELEN   wrecker   HELEN   Hell
the one who first named her knew what was fated –
HEL-   a god guided his tongue right   -EN
HEL-   spear-bride   gore-bride   war-whore   -EN
HEL-   ship-wrecker   man-breaker   Troy-knacker   -EN

To the Chorus, though, 'Helen' is no *non sequitur* to the Herald's doom-tale; indeed, she is synonymous with it, for she is the war's cause and bears the war's blame. (We have to wonder about this though. Isn't Helen a convenient fiction, the name men give to what they intend to do anyway?) Helen is demonised in an act of linguistic deconstruction that works on her as she supposedly works on men: her name is literally taken apart and appropriated to other cultural uses, so that 'Helen' turns into 'Hell' and now serves as the sign predicting her own effect. But the story of the sacrifice of Iphigeneia still rings in our ears: 'the war effort wants it, the war effort gets it'. Isn't Helen just another bit of what the war effort wants to keep its wheels turning?

FROM *The Common Chorus (pages 96-98)*
Harrison made a first adaptation of Aristophanes' *Lysistrata* (which has the women of Athens in 411 BC declaring a sex-strike until their menfolk end the twenty-one year long war with Sparta) when he was living in Africa. *Aikin Mata* (Hausa, = women's work) was written specifically for a group of university student actors whose Ibo, Fulani, Yoruba and Hausa ethnic differences were brought into play in the satire. That first version is a million miles from this second re-vision, called *The Common Chorus*, but as Harrison observes, 'There are fifty ways to translate a play.'

He sets *The Common Chorus* – a title bursting with puns – at Greenham Common at the height of the anti-war protest. Phallic aggression and military aggression are bound together in the language they share on this site: a 'Trojan' is the ancient civilisation, recalled here, that was 'scorched into futureless dustbowls' in *The Oresteia*. But it's also the brand name of an American condom and the secret code name of an American plan to target seventy Soviet cities with nuclear missiles. The soldiers guarding the Greenham site shout obscenities (as they did in real life) at the women pro-testers. Sex and war constantly get mixed up in their "ejaculations". The women retaliate by hanging on the perimeter fence 'home-made improvised' model penises which, says a stage direction, 'might be a cross between traditional Greek phalluses and model Cruise Missiles. The GUARDS stand behind the projecting [phalluses]

160

trying to ignore the fact that they look ridiculous.' The women (as they did in real life) utterly bamboozle the guards by managing to lock the main gate of the base. Harrison makes this a metaphor: 'gate' in Greek is one of Aristophanes' euphemisms for 'vagina'.

The extract is taken from about half way through the play when the Inspector of Police has arrived on the scene to deal with 'Female crime'. And men are to blame for it, he says. 'This is what happens when you treat [women] like an equal': 'they try to castrate us by stopping wars'.

Lysistrata tries to make the Inspector understand what war means in the second half of the twentieth century when we've developed nuclear weapons that can end not just our lives but the planet's life, not just our history but the planet's history: so with Greenham goes Troy, as Poseidon (the sea-borne nuclear missile) destroys Poseidon (the brother-god to Zeus who rules the seas). In the debate about the deployment of these missiles women's opinions are so far marginalised they've dropped off the negotiating table: 'What's it got to do with women anyway?' asks the Inspector. But women can no longer afford to indulge the boys' war games. So Harrison's Lysistrata devises a plan.

She never got to perform it, though. *The Common Chorus*, commissioned by the National Theatre, was never produced. 'By the time various managements had lingered over this text,' writes Harrison in the preface to the published version, the missiles were removed, the cold war put on ice, the Greenham women returned to other lives. So 'my play has been marooned in its moment'.

FROM *Medea: a sex-war opera (pages 99-100)*
Medea (commissioned for the New York Metropolitan Opera in 1985) has yet to be performed as an opera. Harrison's published text is prefaced by a quotation from Claude Levi-Strauss: 'We define the myth as consisting of all its versions'. This opera adds another version of the Medea story onto the layered myth. Harrison constructs his *Medea* partly out of fragments of a number of earlier versions (and in reaction to them).

Medea, daughter of King Aeetes, falls in love with Jason when he comes to Colchis in quest of the Golden Fleece. She uses her power as – what? witch? sorceress? herbalist? – to brew a potion that drugs the dragon that guards the fleece. Jason steals the fleece, and with it, Medea. Jason carries her away. He marries her. They have children. But some years later Jason decides he must make a more advantageous marriage, to Creusa, the daughter of King Creon.

Medea gives the bride a present, a wedding garment steeped in the poison blood of Typhon. When Creusa puts it on it flays the flesh off her bones. Medea exacts further revenge upon Jason. She murders his – her – sons. Except that in Harrison's *Medea* the killing scene is played twice. The first gives the accepted male 'revisionist' version of the story. It makes Medea a monster wielding the knife on her own babies. The replay shows the *original, erased* version, in which *men*, the men of Corinth, do the killing. Harrison's *Medea* uses the story of Hercules as its counter-narrative. At the end, we watch Hercules in his rage slay his children. He batters them to death with his club.

In this extract, which follows the replay of the killing, the Chorus tells the audience to pay attention to who's re-making history and to serve what political agenda. They catalogue the women that male mythology has demonised in order to make women the originators of evil: Helen, daughter of Leda, who "caused" the Trojan War; Eve who "made" Adam eat the apple and so doomed mankind to death; Pandora who opened the box and "released" evil into the world. The Chorus traces the programme by which men supplanted the ancient matriarchal earth gods, whose power of blood and womb they could not control, and replaced them with a new race of male sky gods, whose power is intellectual. No blood. No mess. (So Father Zeus "gives birth" to his daughter Athene, who springs full grown from his forehead. And Euripides, who wrote a version of *Medea*, has his misogynist Jason figure out a way to dispense with women altogether.) We can use Harrison's *Medea: a sex-war opera* to gloss his 'sex-war' *Oresteia*.

FROM *Square Rounds (pages 101-105)*
Harrison wrote *The Oresteia* for an all-male company. 'It has to be played by men,' he says, 'because *The Oresteia* is a male tract. Men have the problems in *The Oresteia* and the plays make them confront them.' By contrast, he wrote *Square Rounds* for women. Both Fritz and Clara in the extract are played by women. Should we, then, consider *Square Rounds* as a "female tract"?

I think so. It's an anti-war play, set at the time of the First World War, that was originally conceived as part of a war trilogy that would include *The Common Chorus* and a Harrison adaptation of Euripides' *The Trojan Women*. In *Square Rounds* and *The Common Chorus* women have the problem, and the plays focus their confrontation of it. The problem is war. War is anti-feminist. For men, war is glory and game: it turns out 'heroes' whose vocabulary of destruction rhymes heroism and "play". In war, men get to wield both the bombast of politics and the military hardware. And what is women's work in war? To find water for their babies. To sift through the rubble to find food. To keep life in bodies. To preserve the rituals of civilisation: washing clothes, teaching children to read, rocking them to sleep in a world that might be gone in the morning. Are these the rituals of futility?

Women have good reason to be anti-war and to interrogate the ways they themselves sponsor war by heroising the men who perpetuate it. *Square Rounds* is an intervention in this debate. It premièred at the National Theatre in October 1992, only months after the Gulf War ended. The play develops a metaphor Harrison introduced in the sonnets – in **Fire-eater**, for example – of the conjuror performing impossible magic tricks. The conjuror of *Square Rounds* is the scientist. The stage s/he performs on, described in the stage directions, is 'A circle of white surrounded by a black circle. It could be read as a "deconstructed" top hat.' The magic the scientist makes is chemical, chemical transformation. And the production itself proceeded as a series of magic illusions. The stage directions read like descriptions of Paul Daniel's magic show, and the credits list 'Ali Bongo' as 'magic consultant'.

In *Square Rounds* the 'magic' science devotes itself to is the invention of ever more efficient weapons of mass destruction: we've come a long way since the pitch-soaked firebrands that burned Troy; via *Square Rounds* we'll get to Lysistrata's nuclear missiles in *The Common Chorus*. Here, we're still thinking about conventional weapons like the Maxim gun. The unrivalled excellence of the Maxim gun (ultimate deterrent, *c.* 1915) was that it fired an automatic, continuous round of 'rounds'. This was an improvement on the Puckle gun (ultimate deterrent, 1719) which had its own high-tech feature. It was designed to preserve race discrimination even in killing. Puckle, a white supremacist, thought white enemies deserved a decent death; the "infidel" was another matter:

> With his Protestant zeal he fashioned the steel
> that got shot from his gun in two forms.
> Paradox though it sounds he fashioned *square rounds*
> to kill those who scorned Christian norms.
>
> If it's the cross you revere you get killed by a sphere
> but if you face toward Mecca at prayer
> the pain that you'll feel pierced by James Puckle's steel
> is redoubled when bullets are square.

We can't help but hear this verse bouncing along like a limerick.

That is precisely its power. The inappropriateness of *that* metre narrating *this* matter is horrible. We recoil. Thus, political critique is bound up in poetic technique. Here is a place where Harrison's meaning resides in poetic form.

In the extract, Clara Haber, herself once a chemist, accuses her husband, the brilliant German experimental chemist Fritz Haber, of betrayal. He's turned his research attention to developing for the Kaiser a weapon he can use against the Maxim gun. He's developing chlorine gas.

> I gave up chemistry to serve you as a wife
> Now you betray our science to poison life.

The logic of Haber's answer – with its appeal to *maternal* feeling! – is chilling. He has a mission to serve 'the Prussians as their Prospero'. He actually believes, like every other deviser of the *ultimate* weapon – which turns out to be the prototype for the next generation of *ultimate* weapons – that *his* ultimate weapon will end the war. *His* ultimate weapon is going to be the agent of peace! Clara stops listening to this nonsense. She blows her brains out.

FROM *The Trackers of Oxyrhynchus (pages 106–110)*

Harrison's *Trackers* is a modern satyr play written around an ancient core: a surviving fragment of a satyr play by Sophocles, *Ichneutae* (= Trackers). Two British papyrologists, Bernard Grenfell and Arthur Hunt, excavating around Oxyrhynchus in Egypt at the turn of the century, discovered the fragment. It was a unique find and remains the only example of Sophocles' work in this kind. Of course Sophocles – like Aeschylus and Euripides, his contemporaries in Athens in the fifth century BC – would have written many satyr plays. The playwriting competition that was the centrepiece of the festival of Dionysus in Athens each year required each of the three contestants to enter a trilogy, three tragedies (like *The Oresteia*) performed on a single day. The cycle of trilogies were then played on consecutive days, and at the end, judges voted the winner.

In fact, however, these trilogies were tetralogies. The fourth play, the end-of-the-day play, was a satyr play, written by the same playwright and using instead of the tragic chorus of Old Men or Libation Bearers or Furies, a chorus of satyrs: half man, half beast, goat-footed, horse-eared, long-tailed. A satyr's most splendid attribute was his enormous erect phallus, and his play, coming after the tragedy (which took men away from the familiar into a consideration of the unknown) returned man to earth, brought him back from his interrogation of the gods to his enjoyment of what connected him to the beasts.

The satyr is raucous and ribald. He gets drunk freely and copulates just as freely. His presence at the end of the tragic day is essential to our understanding of the spirit of Greek theatre, a theatre in which, at the very moment we hear the doom-drum fall silent we hear the satyr's tambourine start to jangle. Greek theatre depends on satyrs. Satyrs are its main supporters. They are the ones who, in the theatre of Dionysus that sits at the foot of the Acropolis, literally carry the stage on their bent-double backs.

But very early on, that satyr-ic spirit was suppressed. Some of the earliest totalitarians of culture systematically (or maybe heedlessly) wiped out the texts of the satyr plays: the scholars who compiled the great library in Alexandria in the third century BC lopped the "low art" satyr plays off from the "high art" tragedies. Only one entire satyr play survives, the *Cyclops* of Euripides. The Sophoclean fragment Grenfell and Hunt discovered on the Oxyrhynchus rubbish tip probably found its way there wrapped around someone's vegetable peelings.

From the fragment's 400 extant lines it is possible to piece together the original story. Apollo, god of the sun, of prophecy, of healing, and of the arts, has lost his cattle. He employs a herd of satyrs – the 'trackers' of the title – led by the superannuated – and phallicly deflated – Silenus, to track them down. They do. Only to discover that the cattle have been slain by the infant Hermes and made into a newfangled gadget, a lyre. Apollo claims the instrument: the moo-sic he makes on its strings is music to his ears.

The new play Harrison writes around this ancient core uses Sophocles (and the fate of Sophocles' satyrs) to cross-reference cultural scenarios he sees being played out today: the way art is divided into 'high' and 'low'; the way culture has been appropriated by the Apollonian elite; the way the mind is privileged over the body, so that the Calibans must always bow and scrape to the Prosperos of art; the way the 'plebs' are excluded from 'patrician' pleasures, access denied them to theatre, music, opera, ballet. But in the extract, Silenus challenges this Apollonian status quo. He contests Apollo's appropriation of the lyre. He details the *satyr*-ic agenda:

> We're not just the clowns sent in to clear the ring
> we're here to show surprise at everything.

A satyr's job is to *wonder* – to hold up the stage – but never to step onto it, never to perform. Silenus breaks the rules. He mounts the stage, and he leads the satyr chorus in a chant that claims culture for 'UZ! UZ! UZ!' But then he retreats: 'We have to keep a proper distance though...' And he tells the story of his brother satyr Marsyas, who aspired to an art the 'nobs' had discarded – and paid for his presumption fearfully. Apollo had him flayed alive. While the business was being done, Apollo stood by, fingering the lyre.

The Marsyas story is tragic in itself, but in Harrison's re-vision, it's also a warning. At the end of *Trackers* the satyrs who've been programmatically excluded from culture by the "nobs" who've appropriated it turn into "yobs". Alienated from culture, they turn into cultural vandals who wreck their own play.

Harrison, following Athenian practice of 2500 years ago, wrote *Trackers* for a *single* performance at the Delphi Festival in 1989. The extract is taken from the Delphi text. In 1990 *Trackers* came to the National Theatre for a brief run. Harrison rewrote the play for London.

FROM *Poetry or Bust (pages 111-113)*
From the first meeting between Harrison and the actors in September 1993, when not a word of this play had been written, it was thirteen days until its first performance. (This is 'immediate poetry', along the lines of **Summoned by Bells** or **Initial Illumination**, poems originally published in *The Guardian* as immediate responses to current affairs.) Harrison wrote *Poetry or Bust* on a challenge. The play was to coincide with the opening of a new David Hockney exhibition at Salts Mill in Bradford, which billed Hockney and Harrison as 'Two Local Artists'.

John Nicholson was the self-proclaimed Airedale poet who aspired to Parnassus (the hill of poetic fame in Greece where the Muses live) but only ever reached Ilkley Moor. His best poetry was stuff he improvised in pubs: he's the poet-as-busker who exemplifies Harrison's belief that poetry belongs to all classes and is generated by all classes. But he betrayed his talent by betraying his own voice, by affecting a "posh" voice in poetry that conformed to some Victorian notion of the "appropriate diction" of poetry. The poetry Nicholson recites in the play – his own – is florid, sentimental, elevated. But the poetry he *speaks* in the play – poetry Harrison writes for him – gives him back his native tongue.

The play's title is a pun. It is reminiscent of the daredevil slogan the settlers painted on their Conestoga wagons as they set off across the Great Plains of America: 'California or Bust', we'll get there or die. (And Nicholson is going to make poetry or die.) But the 'bust' is also the play's literalisation of Nicholson's hunger for fame. In the extract, Nicholson has gone to London to seek immortality (and to visit the famous sculptor, Chantrey, to order his bust). He can't afford marble, just plaster. In London he goes on a bender, tries to flog his poetry to the "posh" patrons of the Covent Garden Opera House, and gets thrown in the slammer for his trouble. When he gets back to Bingley, having poured his fame down his throat but still clutching his 'bundle' of fame, he meets his wife. She too is holding a bundle. It's his baby. She's dead. Presumably, she starved. Nicholson falters. He drops the bust. Being plaster, it breaks.

SECTION FIVE

A Kumquat for John Keats *(pages 114-117)*

Keats has been the ghost-writer in Harrison's poetic life since he was eleven. He is the poet the schoolboy is reciting in **Them &** **[uz]**; he is remembered in **Timer** and **Bringing Up**. Here, Harrison recalls his 'Ode on a Grecian Urn', 'Ode to a Nightingale', and 'Ode to Melancholy': these are the parallel texts that gloss Harrison's **Kumquat**, a poem he addresses partly to the reader, partly to Keats. This poem (says Harrison) 'asks what an undeniable capacity for joy tastes like in a world which is full of pain, misery, despair, hunger and possible extinction'.

'In the very temple of Delight,' says Keats, 'Veiled Melancholy has her sovran shrine.' But Harrison sees more than mere Melancholy dwelling at the centre of Delight. He sees horror there: the shirt of Nessus that burned the skin off Hercules' back is napalm torching a child's body; the thing 'no bigger than an urn' that 'explodes and ravishes all silence' is not Keats' Grecian urn but the atom bomb. It's not just Pain with a capital 'P' that Harrison knows about. He has experienced that kind of pain that makes us know we're mortal and wish we weren't: sitting beside his daughter's hospital bed wondering if she'll live; grieving for his mother's death, her funeral wreaths jostling against the Christmas decorations; suffering 'slings and arrows of outrageous [or even everyday] fortune': whatever it was that caused his 'bile' and 'self-defeat' the year before.

But the kumquat demonstrates how Melancholy dwells *in* Delight, how joy exists in a world the intellect tells you is full of pain. This

> kumquat fruit expresses best
> how days have darkness round them like a rind,
> life has a skin of death that keeps its zest.

We hear in these lines one of the great pleasures of this poem: the way sensuality is reproduced acoustically. We *feel* sound in this poem. And we *feel* the way intellectual connections are made first to our ear, then to our brain, and then the way these connections immediately get transferred and written upon our hearts: days/ darkness, round/rind. So in other lines we feel the sound of 'crunching kumquats'; 'the pith, the pips, the peel'; 'the fruits that were his futures far behind'.

Keats died of consumption aged 26 in 1821, his troubled love affair with Fanny Brawne having brought him mostly pain. The kumquat, coincidentally, was introduced into England via Kew Gardens in 1822. Lemprière's classical dictionary (1788) was standard for many decades. Proserpine (= Greek mythology's Persephone), daughter of Ceres (Demeter), was abducted by Pluto (Hades) and taken to the underworld to be his consort. Naiads and dryads are lesser immortals who live in and give life to streams and woodlands. 'Micanopy' is a small town north of Harrison's Florida retreat, a place he describes as 'a Promethean swampland'.

The poem has an easiness to it that is conveyed by the run-over lines. Its meditative quality is sensual; we feel this poem on the palate and on the fingers' ends as well as on the ears. Keats, too, was a great oral poet. A letter by Keats which Harrison quotes as a gloss upon his own poem has Keats writing the letter with one hand while he holds in the other a nectarine whose juice dribbles over him. 'Good God!' says Keats in the letter, 'how fine!' It is this celebration of the sensual that Harrison wants to share with Keats in offering him the kumquat. But more than that, Harrison's poem is, *inter alia*, a love poem to a lover who is never directly addressed nor identified but whose presence is felt throughout. It is characteristic of Harrison's double vision, his pessimistic intellect bound to his celebratory nature, that **A Kumquat for John Keats** ends with buzzards (birds of death?), with the sound of saws being sharpened (to cut down the tree of life?) and with the recollections of last night's love playing upon the bedsprings whose noise sounds just like Mr. Fowler's (a pun, or just a coincidence?) saws.

The Call of Nature *(page 118)*
D.H. Lawrence (born in Nottinghamshire in 1885, the son of a miner and of a devoted mother who – like Harrison's – wanted her son to be a schoolmaster) got his reputation as the 'priest of sex' from his novels, *Sons and Lovers* (1913), *The Rainbow* (1915) and *Women in Love* (1916). His shocking elopement with a married

woman in 1912 contributed to the imputation of scandal that surrounded his work. *Lady Chatterley's Lover* (1928) multiplied that scandal ten-fold (the book was only finally published in an unexpurgated version in Britain in 1962 after a famous obscenity trial). Lawrence sought relief from scandal and from tubercular infection by retreating to a ranch high in the desert mountains of New Mexico in America. He answered 'the call of nature'.

Sixty years later, tourists bussed in to rubberneck the 'priest of sex' stay on the bus. His 'sex' books aren't ones they're likely to have read. This once-sacred place they are visiting, with its ancestral battlefields and the melting snow mingling with the blood of Christ (= 'Sangre de Cristo') is despoiled. But not by Lawrence's views on sex. Corruption arrives in 'respectable' packaging: capitalism and consumerism corrupt both the people and the place. The Taos landscape is blighted with the junk of a junk culture, the natives play travesties of themselves in films that make them 'bite the dust', and, when the tourists answer their own 'call of nature', they disappear into lavatories that mark culture as kitsch and sexuality as kitsch-ified: 'BRAVES! SQUAWS!'

Remains *(page 119)*

Wordsworth's cottage at Grasmere was the first 'literary property' in Britain to be purchased (by private subscription) with the intention of preserving it in trust for the nation. That is how 'W. Martin paperhanger' came to be writing his graffiti (which he then wallpapered over) on the back of the shutter in the room Coleridge occupied when he visited the Wordsworths: Martin was working for the trust that had bought Dove Cottage and was restoring it for tourists to visit – in 1891! So Wordsworth was already being turned into a bardic national monument within forty years of his death. Harrison reflects upon immortality – he's glancing sideways at Wordsworth's 'Ode on Intimations of Immortality' – but also on mortality. He's thinking about what 'remains' and what doesn't remain, and he honours Martin's one secret – now revealed – line of poetry, his 'one visit by the Muse', its 'five strong verse feet'. It's an accident that this unofficial working-class poet survives in a house that poetry has made a shrine. But it's a suggestive accident. Maybe as we worship at such official shrines we should check behind the shutters for all the other poets who might be standing in the shadows. Harrison dedicates this poem to Robert Woof, the Director of the Wordsworth Trust, and to fellow poet Fleur Adcock, who were with him when he visited Dove Cottage.

On Not Being Milton *(page 120)*

In *Streuwwelpeter*, the gruesomely didactic German children's tales – more grim than Grimm – the schoolboys who call the black boy names are dipped in the inkwell of Dr Agrippa. They're turned black. In his *Cahier d'un retour au pays natal* ('Notebook on a Return to My Native Land') the black Martinican writer, Aimé Césaire – who, as a French speaker in a Caribbean country, knows he speaks the language of the coloniser – celebrates 'negritude'. He discovers black pride in black race consciousness, and he develops a black aesthetics to express black experience. In **On Not Being Milton**, Tony Harrison, with one eye on Dr Agrippa and the other on Césaire, celebrates his own 'negritude'. He dedicates himself to 'growing black enough to fit my boots'.

Harrison spent several years in Africa and another year travelling in Cuba and the Caribbean. There, he saw overt racism. But he also saw black activism working through education and politics to empower and enfranchise the black in a post-colonial world. He dedicates this poem to Vieira and Guebuza as a salute to black activism. Harrison met these two leaders of FRELIMO (which later became Mozambique's Marxist ruling party), in 1971. Along with being guerrilla fighters, the two were poets as well. The dedication likewise signals Harrison's own resolve to keep faith with his discovered 'negritude'. In his life, black consciousness gets translated into class consciousness. He is marked, as surely as if he had dived into Dr Agrippa's inkwell, only not by the colour of his skin but by the sound of his voice. Harrison's struggle politicises art and articulacy in order to discover an aesthetic of language and poetry that can accommodate a voice that emerges out of the working class of Leeds, a city that turned its native sons black with the grime of post-Industrial Revolution urban pollution. (This takes us back to *Biston Carbonaria* in **Art & Extinction**.)

In the middle section of the sonnet, Harrison draws an analogy between art and nineteenth-century industrial militancy. The Luddites smashed the textile machines that deprived them of their livelihoods; so Harrison's Leeds voice will smash the 'frames of Art'. Here, Art with a capital 'A' = owned language. It is language owned by the elite. It is 'forged' – counterfeit – but is going to be 'forged' – made strong – in another sense. So *Harrison* is the stuttering 'scold' (where scold = shrew but also Norse 'skald', 'poet'). *He* is breaking the 'branks of condescension'. (A 'brank' was a scold's bridle: put into her mouth to curb her tongue, it was held in place by a 'frame', another of those 'frames of Art'! In 'brank' we hear the suppressed rhyme 'rank', and we think of rank upon rank of grammar school boys learning Latin conjugations in ranks of verb tables.) Harrison's Leeds voice is going to come down on 'Art' like an Enoch hammer. (Enoch was the man who made both the textile frames and the implement the Luddites used to smash them: their cry was 'Enoch made them, Enoch shall break them!') Of course, the phrase 'frames of Art' was originally John Milton's, writing in the seventeenth century. 'Frames' means 'forms' and it was Milton, imitating (like Harrison) Greek and Latin poetic masters, who 'framed' – made, constructed – the 'frames' – forms – of poetry that have been our models ever since. Are these the 'frames' that Harrison intends to smash? How do we read the double potential of the title that declares **On** *Not* **Being Milton?**

Harrison's battle cry goes up: 'Three cheers for mute ingloriousness'. The political observation underpinning that cry comes in the next line: 'Articulation is the tongue-tied's fighting.' The suppression of language = the suppression of people. The poet is there to resist such suppression. 'Who owns language?' asks the poet. 'Who owns history?'

Questions like these make expression a political *as well as* a cultural activity. But such 'activity' is ambiguous for a poet: *silence,* not activity, is the necessary surround to poetry. If 'mute ingloriousness' is given 'three cheers' here, it was certainly not applauded in the original poem from which Harrison borrowed the phrase. Thomas Gray's *Elegy* (1750) mourned the 'mute inglorious Milton' who had died in poetic silence. *His* silence was unrealised potential.

Harrison's **Milton** can be read as a gloss on all his other poetry. It is both a summary and an introduction; it is a "brief " of his poetic technique. It takes us back to his beginning. It bids us to ask questions: is the analogy between political and linguistic violence valid? How do we make sense of this paradox (particular to this poem but relevant to all Harrison's poetry): Harrison's celebration of the inarticulate is itself 'framed', and in a high-literary manner. Does it exclude those whose interests it purports to serve? Or does it rather show that articulation is always going to be in tension with silence? Richard Tidd, the shoemaker, gives us an answer. He was executed for his participation in a conspiracy, planned at Cato Street in 1820, to assassinate the Cabinet. Tidd's final comment speaks out of (and to) his own experience. But we can 'frame' it differently. For it usefully places the poet's work in culture, and usefully ironises it:

Sir, I Ham a very Bad Hand at Righting.

FURTHER READING

This bibliography aims to extend your reading of Harrison by guiding you to more of his poetry and to more writing about that poetry. It is arranged chronologically and of course includes his theatre and film poetry. A longer annotated bibliography, current to 1991, can be found in Neil Astley's anthology, *Tony Harrison*, cited below. The critics, academics and poets I quote in my Introduction can be tracked down to their contributions in the Astley anthology.

Primary Reading

The Loiners (London Magazine Editions, 1970). Harrison's first book-length collection.

U.S. Martial (Bloodaxe Books, 1981). Pamphlet of poems by the Latin poet Martial rendered into New York vernacular; reissued in 1989.

The Oresteia. Television film of the 1982 National Theatre production directed by Peter Hall; first shown on Channel 4 on 9 October 1983.

Selected Poems (Penguin Books, 1984; second edition, 1987). Expands *The School of Eloquence* sonnets (first published as ten, then eighteen, then fifty poems) to sixty-seven sonnets. The first section includes poems from *The Loiners*. The nine previously uncollected poems at the end are mostly set in America and include 'A Kumquat for John Keats'.

V. (Bloodaxe Books, 1985). First edition published in hardback and paperback, containing the whole poem with fourteen photographs by Graham Sykes.

The Mysteries (Faber, 1985). The complete trilogy of plays from the York, Wakefield, Chester and Coventry Mystery Cycles, devised by Harrison with the National Theatre Company and first performed as a trilogy in the Cottesloe Theatre on 19 January 1985. (*The Passion* – Part II of the eventual trilogy – was originally performed at the Cottesloe in 1977; *Nativity* – Part 1 – opened at the 1980 Edinburgh Festival and then transferred to the Cottesloe.) Bill Bryden directed all the plays.

Dramatic Verse 1973-1985 (Bloodaxe Books, 1985). This edition includes the complete texts of *The Misanthrope, Phaedra Britannica, Bow Down, The Bartered Bride, The Oresteia, Yan Tan Tethera, The Big H* and *Medea: a sex-war opera*.

Theatre Works 1973-1985 (Penguin Books, 1986). Paperback edition of *Dramatic Verse 1973-1985* with a different title.

V. (Bloodaxe Books, 1989). Second edition published after the controversy over Channel 4's film of the poem. It contains the whole poem plus 35 press items – letters to newspapers, the House of Commons motion attacking the film of the poem, articles from tabloid and "quality" papers as well as a defence of the poem and the film by director Richard Eyre and a transcript of the phone calls logged by Channel 4 on the night of the broadcast.

V. and Other Poems (Farrar Straus Giroux, New York, 1990). Harrison's second American book of poems. It includes eight 'Sonnets for August 1945' and six other previously uncollected poems: 'The Act', 'Y', 'Summoned by Bells', 'The Pomegranates of Patmos', 'Broadway' and 'The Mother of the Muses', as well as *V.*

The Trackers of Oxyrhynchus (Faber, 1990). The first edition contains the 1988 Delphi text; the second edition in 1991 published both the Delphi text and the 1990 Olivier text, the revision Harrison made when *Trackers* came to the National Theatre. Both editions are prefaced by Harrison's introductions.

The Common Chorus (Faber, 1992). Originally the working title of a trilogy of war plays to be performed by women, *The Common Chorus* came to stand as the published title of the single play Harrison originally titled *Lysistrata*. Set at Greenham Common, this play has yet to be performed professionally. It is prefaced by Harrison's introduction, 'Hecuba to Us'.

Square Rounds (Faber, 1992). Originally titled *Maxims* and intended as the third play in *The Common Chorus* trilogy, *Square Rounds* was reworked into a separate play and performed at the National Theatre in 1992.

The Gaze of the Gorgon (Bloodaxe Books, 1992). This contains Harrison's television poem, first shown on BBC 2 on 3 October 1992, which uses the Gorgon as a metaphor for the horrors of modern warfare. It also collects the 'Sonnets for August 1945', 'A Cold Coming' and 'The Mother of the Muses' together with a dozen more poems.

Black Daisies for the Bride (Faber, 1993). First broadcast by BBC 2 on 30 June 1993.

The Shadow of Hiroshima and Other Film Poems (Faber, 1995).

Secondary Reading

Neil Astley (editor): *Tony Harrison* (Bloodaxe Books, 1991). Essential reading. This anthology contains eight essays and prefaces by Harrison; reviews of his poetry and plays; articles by directors, designers and actors; critical essays and articles by poets, academics and critics; interviews with Harrison; the complete texts of *The Blasphemers' Banquet*, *Arctic Paradise*, and 'The Mother of the Muses'; annotated bibliography and chronology.

Richard Hoggart: *The Uses of Literacy: Aspects of Working-Class Life* (Chatto, 1957; available as Penguin paperback). The classic account of the formation of working-class identity through popular literary forms.

Luke Spencer: *The Poetry of Tony Harrison* (Harvester Books, 1994). Uneven and largely unreadable. Constantly misreads Harrison.

E.P. Thompson: *The Making of the English Working Class* (Gollancz, 1963, available as Penguin paperback).

BIOGRAPHICAL NOTE

Tony Harrison was born in Leeds in 1937. At the age of eleven he won a scholarship to Leeds Grammar School. From there, he went to Leeds University where he took a degree in Classics and began Ph.D. research on Virgil's *Aeneid*. He spent four years in West Africa and a year in Prague before returning to Britain to become the first Northern Arts Literary Fellow in 1967, a post he again held in 1976-77. A UNESCO Fellowship in 1968 took him to Cuba, Brazil, Senegal and the Gambia; the following year, his first book of poetry, *The Loiners*, was published. It was awarded the Geoffrey Faber Memorial Prize in 1972 and brought Harrison to the attention of the theatre director, John Dexter, who commissioned from him a re-vision of Molière's *Misanthrope* for the National Theatre in 1973. Harrison has been writing for the theatre ever since.

His version of Aeschylus's *Oresteia* won him the European Poetry Translation Prize in 1982. His collection, *The Gaze of the Gorgon*, won the Whitbread Poetry Prize in 1993. His television film, *Black Daisies for the Bride*, won the Prix Italia in 1994. Harrison lives in Newcastle upon Tyne.